TONIE AND VALMAI HOLT

Germany Awake!

THE RISE OF NATIONAL SOCIALISM: 1919-1939

ILLUSTRATED BY THE
CONTEMPORARY PICTURE POSTCARD

LONGMAN • LONDON AND NEW YORK

Longman Group Limited
Longman House, Burnt Mill, Harlow
Essex CM20 2JE, England
Associated companies throughout the world

Published in the United States of America
by Longman Inc., New York

First published 1986

British Library Cataloguing in Publication Data
Holt, Tonie
   Germany awake!: the rise of National
   Socialism 1919–1939.
   1. Postal cards – Germany – History –
   20th century 2. Germany – Politics and
   government – 1918–1933 3. Germany –
   Politics and government – 1933–1945
   I. Title II. Holt, Valmai
   769′.49943085   DD237
   ISBN 0-582-40619-6

Library of Congress Cataloging in Publication Data
Holt, Tonie.
   Germany awake!

   Includes index.
   1. Germany – History – 1918–1933 – Pictorial works.
  2. Germany – History – 1933–1945 – Pictorial works.
  3. Postal cards – Germany. I. Holt, Valmai. II. Title.
  DD237.H59 1985   943.085   84-20132
  ISBN 0-582-40619-6

Set in Linotron 202 11/13 pt. Bembo Roman
Produced by Longman Group (FE) Limited
Printed in Hong Kong

Contents

Chronology

This list is intended to serve as a simple *aide-memoire*. It forms a skeleton chronological framework which has dictated the sequence in which the postcards are illustrated, and around which the captions and chapters in the book are written.

Introduction
1869	1	Oct.	The world's first postcard issued in Austria
1882	—	—	The world's first photographic postcard claimed in Nuremberg
1889	20	Apr.	Adolf Hitler born
1906	—	—	Hitler studies painting in Vienna
1912	—	—	Hitler spends six months in Liverpool
1913	—	—	Hitler lives in Munich

First World War
1914	—	—	Hitler volunteers for the army
			Hitler wins Iron Cross Second Class
			Heinrich Hoffmann appointed war photographer
1916	—	—	Hitler wounded
1918	—	—	Hitler wins Iron Cross First Class
	—	Oct.	Hitler gassed
	11	Nov.	First World War ends
	—	—	Hitler returns to Munich as a 'spy'

The Road to the Reich Chancellery
1919	—	—	'Civil war' in Germany
	—	—	Hitler spies on a German Workers' Party meeting at the Sterneckerbrau Bierkeller
	—	—	Hitler joins the German Workers' Party
	—	—	Hitler begins *Bierkeller* speeches
	—	—	Karl Liebknecht's Spartakists fail to seize power
	—	—	Frederick Ebert becomes first President of the Weimar Republic
1920	—	—	Hitler changes party name to National Socialist German Workers' Party (Nazis)
	—	—	Hitler sets out the Nazi philosophy including forfeiture of citizenship by Jews and the abolition of the Treaty of Versailles
1922	—	Nov.	Benito Mussolini becomes Italian dictator
1923	11	Jan.	Belgians and French occupy the Ruhr
	27	Jan.	First Nazi 'Party Day' in Munich

—	Sept.	Hitler's first official Hoffmann photograph
—	Sept.	First Nationalist *Deutscher Tag* in Nuremberg
8/9	Nov.	Munich *putsch*
23	Nov.	Nazi Party banned
1924 —	Apr.	Hitler sent to Landsberg prison
20	Dec.	Hitler released
1925 27	Feb.	Hitler revives the Nazis with a speech at the Burgerbraukeller
—	Apr.	Hindenburg elected President
—	July	*Mein Kampf* published
—	Aug.	Belgians and French leave the Ruhr
9	Nov.	Formation of SS announced
—	—	French begin construction of the Maginot Line
1926 3	July	First 'Blood Flag' party rally in Weimar
1927 19	Aug.	'Day of Awakening' rally at Nuremberg
1929 1	Aug.	'Party Day of Consolidation' rally at Nuremberg
1930 23	Feb.	Death of Horst Wessel
1931 —	Dec.	Five million unemployed in Germany
1932 —	Feb.	World disarmament conference
13	April	SA and SS banned

Triumph of the Will

1933 30	Jan.	Hitler becomes Chancellor
27	Feb.	Reichstag burns down
21	Mar.	Hitler opens his first Reichstag in Potsdam
26	April	Goering founds the Gestapo
—	June	Trade unions abolished
1	July	Germany becomes a one-party State (Nazi)
14	Sept.	'Day of Victory' rally at Nuremberg
—	Oct.	Germany withdraws from the League of Nations
—		*Reichsarbeitsdienst* (RAD) formed
1934 14	Jun.	Hitler and Mussolini meet for the first time
30	Jun.	SA purged in 'Night of the Long Knives'
2	Aug.	Hindenburg dies. Hitler becomes Führer
10	Sept.	'Triumph of Will' rally Nuremberg
1935 13	Jan.	Over 90 per cent of Saar electorate vote to join Germany
10	Sept.	'Day of Freedom' rally at Nuremberg
3	Oct.	Italy invades Ethiopia

The birth of the Axis

1936 7	Mar.	Rhineland occupied by Germany
9	May	Ethiopia annexed by Italy
18	July	Spanish Civil War begins
1	Aug.	Berlin Olympic Games open
8	Sept.	'Day of Honour' rally at Nuremberg
27	Oct.	Berlin–Rome 'Axis' formed
1937 18	July	House of German Art opened
6	Sept.	'Day of Work' rally at Nuremberg
13	Oct.	Germany guarantees Belgian neutrality

It's that man again

1938 12	Nov.	Austria (South Tyrol) occupied by Germany
5	Sept.	'Day of Greater Germany' rally at Nuremberg
30	Sept	Munich Agreement
1	Oct.	Sudetenland occupied by Germany
1939 15	Mar.	Bohemia and Moravia occupied by Germany
23	Mar.	Memel occupied by Germany
28	Mar.	Spanish Civil War ends
1	Sept.	Poland invaded by Germany

The beginning of the Second World War

These maps show the territories taken away from Germany by the Treaty of Versailles. Hitler rallied the German people around him by saying that he would get the territories back.

How Germany was punished at Versailles

Map of the new German frontiers as laid down in the Peace Treaty. Vertically striped areas are those restored to France and Poland or, like the Saar coalfield, taken from Germany. Danzig is a free city. The dotted portions are those in which the inhabitants will vote whether to remain German or not. The shaded portions show the area east of the Rhine in which all forts have to be destroyed, and also the territory on the west bank to be occupied by the Allies for fifteen years as a guarantee.

The fate of Germany's colonial empire

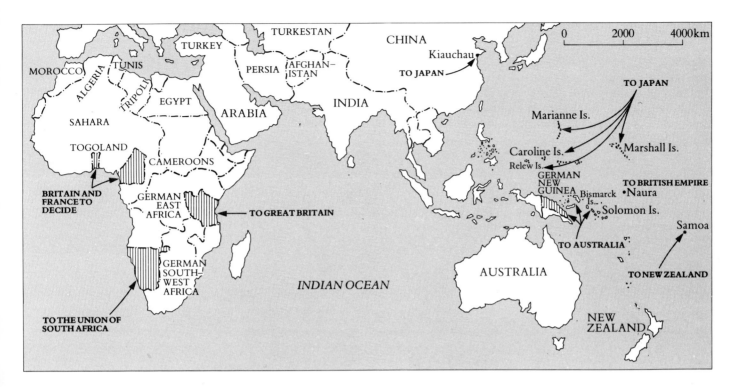

How the Peace Conference divided the captured German colonies. Mandates were given as shown above.

Key to postcard valuations

A: under £2

B: £2–£8

C: £8–£15

D: £15 and over

Acknowledgements

We wish to thank Michael Clarke of 'Desiderata', W. Germany, and Peter Rickenback of London for supplying elusive cards at impossible notice; Frank Coe for his translations of cryptic German messages and captions; Deal, Dover and Canterbury Libraries for promptly answering telephone queries; Vivienne and Wendy for deciphering and typing our sometimes impossible drafts; Paul Kords and Henry Stoller in Munich and 'Pedro' in Berchtesgaden.

Introduction

▼━━━━━▼

It is now more than forty years since the beginning of the Second World War. To those of us who lived through that grim, yet often exhilarating time, it seems unbelievable that half of our present population has been born since 1945 and so has no first-hand experience or knowledge of the war at all.

Historians present their versions of this conflict to the young through the syllabuses of CSE, 'O' and 'A' Levels and degrees – together with the First World War. But the conventional historian exercises retrospective judgement on the events of the past. Actions are analysed, results codified, battles judged as victories or losses. The historian uses his knowledge of wider issues to reflect upon the thoughts and deeds of those who lived in the past and his words are isolated from what actually took place, not from lack of understanding, but simply by the passage of time.

It need not be that way. There is available a virtually untapped contemporary source of words and pictures – the postcard.

In the past decade there has been a widespread interest in things past – the label is 'nostalgia'. At first this was merely an extension of an interest in antiques. Soon, however, with the falling value of money, everyone wanted to collect something old in the hope that it would retain its value, and with the fast-increasing demand, the range of collectable items expanded. Victoriana became popular, then Edwardiana, and now even the Kitsch-style of the 1920s and 1930s is an accepted collecting area.

The nostalgia theme was picked up by the entertainment media and some fine and successful films (like *Yanks*) and television series (like *Upstairs, Downstairs* and *We'll Meet Again*) were made, each one awakening an ever-increasing public interest in the near past.

One Edwardian phenomenon which was revived was the collecting of old picture postcards. At the turn of the century the picture postcard was the newspaper, radio, television and picture magazine of the period. It recorded absolutely everything. It had its own artists, its own terminology, its own postal rate, and, above all, it carried messages. So many cards were produced that contemporary writers voiced the fear that, 'Europe will be drowned in a sea of postcards'. Everyone, royalty included, not only sent postcards, but also collected them.

The modern nostalgic hunt for these old cards grew apace, following an exhibition put on by the Victoria and Albert Museum in 1971. By the mid-1970s, international postcard dealing was established in its own right, and major auction houses such as Sotheby's, Christies and Phillips, listed picture postcards in their catalogues. A major accolade was bestowed on the hobby in 1981 with the publication of the first Stanley Gibbons Postcard Catalogue, and, during the inflation years of the late 1970s and early 1980s, picture postcards kept their values, while collectables in general did not. There is more to the picture postcard than meets the eye of the casual observer.

Unlike a formal picture designed to hang upon a wall for reflective viewing or a photograph intended to supplement a newspaper article, the small canvas of the postcard must capture and present just the essence of its subject as a pictorial précis. This generally plain and simple presentation enables the viewer to come quickly and easily to the point of the picture, a quality which allows the postcard to reach a mass audience. It also identifies the postcard as an ideal propaganda medium, of which the Nazis made great use. But the postcard is also a very personal document, which can carry a written message from one human being to another, and the message may, or may not, deliberately relate to the picture on the card. Picture and message, intentionally or otherwise, separately and jointly, form a unique contemporary record of the period during which they were created, and it is this 'personal time capsule' aspect of the postcard, a sort of peeking behind the net curtains of the past, that is the secret of its fascination.

The cards are valuable too, their catalogue values deriving from a mixture of philatelic attraction and competitive collecting in a market in which supplies are finite and limited. Individual cards have fetched over £1,000, and average prices for collectable examples are measured in pounds rather than in pence. Despite all of this attention, however, and the development of excellent specialist magazines such as the *Picture Postcard Monthly*, knowledge of the social significance of the postcard remains shallow. It offers a challenging opportunity for the energetic historian.

At present, social research is mostly confined to photographic cards detailing the life and times of Victorian and Edwardian Britain, with a parallel situation in France, America and all the countries throughout the world in which postcard collecting was once a national mania. Photographers like Francis Frith and Louis Levy produced series after series of excellent scenes which are enthusiastically collected, but the interest of present-day collectors drops exponentially in anything produced after 1918. It is popularly supposed that with the advent of radio, illustrated newspapers and magazines for mass consumption, coupled with the doubling of postcard postage to 1*d.* at the end of the First World War, the postcard dropped dead. It almost did.

It recovered, however, during the Second World War. The shortage of newsprint, the need to be economical in all things, the requirement for cheap, readily disseminated propaganda, revived the postcard in all the involved nations. The cards are not easy to find because they were not collected and prized in albums as the Edwardian cards had been, but they can be found. And, like their predecessors, they provide a vivid record of the past.

In this volume we follow the chronological development of the period between the two world wars, and look at the Nazi and Axis personalities who shaped the events of those years and of the war-time period which followed. Later volumes will examine the fighting on land, at sea and in the air; the humour, the patriotism and the propaganda. The variety of the cards is astonishing in style, subject matter and quality, and the majority of the illustrations here are from postcards issued between 1919 and 1939.

Our definition of picture postcard is quite precise – it is a card purposely designed, and correctly printed, for transmission through the post at postcard rate. Every picture in this book, with its overt or covert message, was visible to the sender, the recipient and the postal workers who handled it, as well as those who looked at it in the shop but did not buy. Often, successful cards would be repeatedly reprinted, either for plain commercial reasons or continually to reinforce a propaganda message. The Germans were enthusiastic users of the postcard and excelled in dramatic, if restrained (compared to the Italians), presentation, using uniforms and insignia to full effect. The strong Nazi symbols contain a hint of hidden menace that ensures they are taken seriously.

The world's first postcard was issued (without a picture) in Austria on 1 October 1869. By the turn of the century the coloured, artist-drawn, picture card was firmly established and, soon afterwards, the photographic postcard, recording people and events, made its appearance. During the First World War, card production in all the belligerent countries reached its greatest heights, and in a previous book, *Till the Boys Come Home* (Macdonald and Jane's) we illustrated the rich variety of pictures that chronicle that gigantic struggle. That war ended in 1918, and a young German soldier who, like the postcard, was born in Austria, returned to civilian life to begin a political career.

In Part One of this book we follow that career, until politics turn into the First World War. There are the armed struggles of Weimar Germany, the *Bierkeller* political meetings, the peace movements, the Nazis, the parades, the 1936 Olympic Games, the Spanish Civil War, the Italian conquests in Africa and the farce of Munich, 1938. Then, in Part Two, there are the personalities, the politicians and the soldiers, the German people themselves, all of whom are bit players on a world stage dominated by that one German ex-soldier – Adolf Hitler..

1

2

1. The world's first postcard

Austrian postal authorities issued this card on 1 October 1869. Its postage rate was 2 *Kreuzer* (half the cost of a letter) and it carried a pre-printed stamp showing the head of Emperor Franz-Josef. It measured 122×88 mm.

2. Hitler's birthplace, Braunau

Braunau is a small, pretty town on the banks of the River Inn, not far from Munich and Salzburg. The house on the right is where Hitler was born and is today the town library. Federal German authorities had difficulty in the early 1980s with neo-Nazis, who placed flowers outside the house each year on Hitler's birthday. The view has changed very little since the card was published. Even the tree looks the same.

Pub. Franz Hanfstaengel, Munich. Artist Willy Scholz. *Circa* 1930. Value B.

Part One

▼—————▼

1. Mai
Tag der Nationalen Arbeit

The First World War 1914-1919

On 28 June 1914, Archduke Franz Ferdinand, heir to the Austro-Hungarian throne, and his wife, were assassinated in Sarajevo by Serbian students. As a result, Austro-Hungary declared war upon Serbia (now part of Yugoslavia), and through a series of treaties and alliances, nations gathered into two opposing camps. The main protagonists were Austria and Germany, against Britain, France and Russia (the Allies).

On 4 August 1914 Germany began an invasion of France through neutral Belgium, and the British Expeditionary Force was sent to the Continent. The German advance swept to the gates of Paris, but there it faltered, and the invading armies were pushed back north. By the end of the year, following a horrific battle in Flanders (known as 'First Ypres' to the British, and the 'Massacre of the Innocents' to the Germans) in which there were over a quarter of a million casualties, both sides began to dig in. The dramatic increase in firepower produced by the widespread use of the machine gun, and its domination of the open battlefield, led to confronting systems of earth-works and trenches which stretched from the North Sea to Switzerland. This was the Western Front.

Over the next four .years the nations sheltered behind their trenches and sallied forth at intervals in the hope of breaking through the enemy's lines. The conflict became not just a struggle between soldiers, but a contest between capitalist and socialist ideologies, and the will of the civilian populations to continue the conflict.

On the Western Front, many young men served an apprenticeship in warfare, whose lessons later directed their lives, and the lives of millions of others. Among these apprentices were Winston Churchill, Bernard Law Montgomery, Henri Pétain, Charles de Gaulle, Erwin Rommel, George S. Patton and Adolf Hitler.

At the beginning of 1918, the last year of the First World War, socialist-inspired workers' strikes were spreading throughout Germany, and by the end of January 1½ million men were refusing to work. They demanded an honourable end to the war and the democratisation of the Hohenzollern régime. Although Kaiser Wilhelm and the Chief of Army Staff, Eric Ludendorff, were concerned by the strikes, the peace treaty signed in March with Russia meant that Germany now had to wage war on only one front, and the military opportunity this offered for an all-out offensive in France, took priority in their minds. Thus they massed their forces on the Western Front.

On 21 March 1918 the *Kaiserschlacht* (Kaiser's Battle) began. Ludendorff launched his concentrated forces towards Amiens and Paris, and for a while Germany rejoiced in what seemed to be inevitable victory. But it was not to be, and the Allied counter attacks beginning in July recovered all the recently lost territory. Then the Allies began to advance. Germany sued for peace. The Kaiser abdicated and on the same day the German High Seas Fleet at Kiel refused to sail against the British. The mutinous sailors formed themselves into Russian-style soviets (councils) and their action was quickly imitated across

Germany in reaction to the anticlimax of defeat and the departure of the Kaiser.

Socialist organisations manoeuvred for power, and many of the twenty-five different German states which had made up Imperial Germany, struggled to maintain control of law and order by using locally-raised armed forces to discipline mutineers and strikers. Moderate Socialists fought for survival against extreme left-wing Bolsheviks, and, fearing the repetition of the Revolution which had taken place in Russia, they enlisted the help of the Army. But insurrections continued to spring up even after the Armistice, and it was only with the help of the paramilitary forces like the ultra right-wing *Freikorps* that the German Communist Party was defeated in both the political and the military sense, with hundreds of people being killed.

When the war had begun Hitler, then an impecunious artist, had volunteered and joined the 16th Bavarian Reserve Infantry Regiment. He became a runner (a message carrier) and by October 1914 he was in the Flanders area, where he took part in the First Battle of Ypres. Throughout the war he remained a runner, a particularly dangerous job, and earned promotion to corporal. His time in the trenches made a vivid and lasting impression upon him and through the horrors and hardships of the front line he served with courage, winning four decorations including the Iron Cross First Class.

Hitler did not escape the war without injury. He was wounded and then, later on, was gassed, and it was while he was recovering from the effect of the gas that he learned of the Armistice of 11 November 1918.

The Armistice, or cease-fire, had come into effect at the eleventh hour on the eleventh day of the eleventh month. With the signing of the peace treaty at Versailles on 28 June the following year, the Allies imposed severe punishments upon Germany. Apart from enormous financial penalties, and limitations placed on the future strengths of her armed forces, Germany was made to forfeit all of her colonies. Among the penalties were:

Alsace Lorraine	– ceded to France
Malmedy area	– to Belgium
Posen and West Prussia	– to Poland
Danzig	– to be a free city – under the League of Nations
Saar / Schleswig / East Prussia	– to hold a plebiscite after fifteen years to decide if they wished to return to Germany
Rhineland	– to be demilitarised (later occupied by the Allies because of Germany's failure to pay war reparations)

The extreme nature of the penalties placed upon Germany gave many observers a feeling of unease. Instead of providing a just and conciliatory peace, it seemed to some that the treaty terms would serve as a focus for German resentment. They were right. In later years Hitler sought and obtained international sympathy for his campaign to revoke the treaty terms, a campaign that eventually culminated in the recommencement of the First World War under its new name – the Second World War.

3. Hitler in the field

This card purports to show Adolf Hitler (extreme left wearing a *Pickelhaube* helmet) in a dug-out in Flanders during December 1914. Many authoritative historical works show this picture, but its origin is obscure. Hitler was certainly in the area and took part in the First Battle of Ypres, a brief memory of which is contained in *Mein Kampf* (My Struggle). He said of his young companions, 'they knew how to die like old soldiers'. The German caption on the reverse says, 'Adolf Hitler as duty orderly with the 16th (List) Bavarian Reserve Infantry Regiment, Flanders, December 1914'.

German: Pub. Andelfinger, Munich. *Circa* 1925. Value D.

3

The Road to the Reich Chancellery 1919-1933

As the First World War came to an end, so did the German monarchy. Kaiser Wilhelm II abdicated and a Republic was quickly proclaimed. It was just one more of the political changes that throughout Europe were ushering in the age of democracy. But what sort of Republic was it to be? Street power in Germany was firmly in the hands of the army, which still retained a core of armed and well-trained men. But the military knew that, for some years at least, while the victorious Allies remained in a position to oversee the country, their way back to national power must lie along a political road.

Thus, through soldiers acting as political spies, the army kept its eyes open for a political party that it could use as a suitable vehicle for its planned journey back to the level of authority it had enjoyed under the Kaiser. Through a spy named Adolf Hitler it found such a vehicle – the German Workers' Party (DAP). Secretly, the army channelled funds to Hitler and the DAP but meanwhile there was the question of law and order.

When the Republic was proclaimed in November 1918, the army quickly decided to support the moderate socialist government instituted at Weimar under President Friedrich Ebert. At first the major problem was to overcome the growing and vociferous Communist Party, which had sprung out of the extreme left-wing Spartakist movement. Supported by Russian advice, and inspired by the revolution which had toppled the Russian tsar, the communists planned to have their own revolution in Germany.

Ebert's moderate socialists forestalled the communist revolution by calling upon the army to use its power in support of the government. This the army did, but in Berlin and in Munich in particular, it could only achieve local superiority over the armed communists by enlisting the help of the ultra right-wing *Freikorps*. After bloody struggles in those two cities, and in others throughout Germany and Austria, the Communist Party was effectively destroyed, but as a side-effect the Freikorps gained in strength and ambition.

After a short honeymoon period of co-operation between army and 'Freikorps', the latter tried to have its own revolution in Berlin in March 1920. Two 'Freikorps' brigades wearing swastikas on their helmets marched on the city, and although their take-over was defeated by a socialist-inspired general strike, the ease of their short-lived take-over of Berlin prompted the army to assume power in Munich. In a move to co-ordinate activities in Munich and Berlin, the army sent their Adolf Hitler to the capital. Although he arrived too late to take any active part in the proceedings he noted the swastikas for future use, and became obsessed with the idea that the way to power lay through an uprising in Munich followed by a march on Berlin.

Through well-planned and carefully orchestrated meetings in Munich's beer cellars (*Bierkellers*), Hitler began to increase the DAP's following. In an attempt to widen its popular appeal he changed its name to the National Socialist German Workers' Party (NSDAP), which later gained the shortened form of 'Nazi' party. In the summer of 1920, after his return from Berlin, he introduced the swastika as the party's emblem, and its solid black form within a white circle on a blood-red background created a dramatic flag that rallied party members.

By 1923 Hitler felt strong enough to follow his obsession with a German revolution that was to begin in Munich, and from his headquarters in the Burgerbraukeller set out on 9 November with his brownshirt storm troopers to take over the city. As they marched towards the *Feldherrnhalle* (Field Marshals' Hall) building in the centre of Munich, led by the First World War soldier, General Ludendorff, they were fired upon by the police. The would-be revolutionaries scattered and the attempted coup collapsed.

Hitler was put on trial in February 1924, but his powers of oratory were such that he gained the propaganda victory by making himself appear to be the potential saviour of the working people. He was sentenced to five years' imprisonment in Landsberg prison, but served only nine months. While he was there he began to write his memoirs, which were later published by Max Amann a one-time sergeant-major in his old regiment. The memoirs came to be known collectively as *Mein Kampf*.

During Hitler's time in prison, the Nazi Party had declined in membership and authority. Hitler set about rebuilding it. All of his actions carried the aspect of legality, but brute force always remained available. The *Sturmabteilung* (the SA Brownshirts) which had developed from the chuckers-out who maintained order at party meetings, was absorbed into the party structure to come under political control, and a bodyguard unit named the *Schutzstaffel* (the SS Blackshirts), with direct loyalty to Adolf Hitler, was created. But for almost five years the Nazis had to be content to operate only as a local party without a national identity.

In 1929 Hitler gained the support of a chain of national newspapers, and began developing contacts among wealthy businessmen, who believed that they could use him for their own ends. They, like the Army, which had had the same idea, would find that the Nazis wanted only their money and support for as long as it suited them. These contacts provided funds from which the Munich headquarters was equipped and staffed with permanent party officials (*Gauleiter*). Now the Nazi apparatus was beginning to develop the strength that would enable it to challenge the established rule.

As the depression deepened, the Weimar government looked shakier and shakier. Hitler travelled furiously from place to place, speaking out loudly against Weimar policies and identifying the causes of Germany's problems with the Jews and the communists. He rallied army support to his side by promoting the *Dolchstosslegende* (the stab in the back), that had begun to circulate as early as 1919, i.e. the German army had *not* been defeated in battle, it was socialist strikes which had brought Germany down.

In 1930 the government fell into disarray. Field Marshal von Hindenburg, the President, appointed a Chancellor, Heinrich Bruning, with whom he tried to run the country by decree, over-ruling the authority of the *Reichstag* (Parliament). As the control of national affairs drained away from the elected authorities, so the membership of paramilitary organisations swelled and street violence grew.

In the national election of July 1932, the Nazis polled the largest number of votes of all parties, but von Hindenburg declined to invite Hitler to be Chancellor. The Nazis called upon their supporters, particularly the industrialists Krupp, Siemens and Thyssen, to put pressure upon Hindenburg. Massive rallies were staged to gain popular support and Goebbels supervised the production of enormous quantities of Nazi propaganda material. Even the army implied that it would support Hitler's appointment, and eventually, on 30 January 1933, Hindenburg gave in and Hitler became Chancellor. The Nazi reign of terror was nigh!

FÜR FREIHEIT UND RECHT

KURT EISNER, Bayerischer Ministerpräsident

4

Straßenkämpfe in Berlin.
Artillerie-Volltreffer im Marstall.

5

Straßenkämpfe in Berlin.
Das zerstörte Gebäude des
„Berliner Tageblatts"

6

November 1918 he declared Bavaria to be a Republic, and became its first Prime Minister. Following the Armistice, which came four days later, he became a vocal proponent of Bavarian independence and German war guilt. Although Hitler was at that time still a junior NCO in the army, there can be little doubt that Eisner's actions fuelled the future dictator's hatred of the Jews. In February 1919 Eisner was assassinated, and further armed uprisings in Munich led to the socialist-inspired 'red terror', and in reaction, the formation of the right-wing Freikorps.

The 'red' terror was then replaced by a 'white' one.

German: Pub. Ludwig Welsch, Munich. 1918. Value C.

5. Street fighting in Berlin – artillery fire

On 6 January 1919 the extreme left, including Karl Lieb-knecht's Spartakists, called for an armed revolution. Almost a quarter of a million people responded, including members of the People's Naval Division, which had been formed from the mutinous sailors of Kiel. Badly organised, the rebellion collapsed, although there was street fighting for several days and many of the revolutionaries were summarily executed.

German: Pub. Willi Ruge, Berlin. 1919. Value B.

6. Street fighting in Berlin – the damaged newspaper building

During the January 1919 Spartakist uprising the *Berliner Tageblatts* (Berlin Daily News) newspaper building was taken over by the revolutionaries and bombarded by guns manned by the army. The latter was assisted by elements of the right-wing Freikorps, who greatly outnumbered them. These irregular forces, less disciplined than the army, exacted brutal revenge on the socialists and indulged in indiscriminate killing.

German: Pub. Ange Photochemie, Berlin. 1919. Value B.

4. Kurt Eisner, Bavarian Prime Minister

A German Jew, born in Berlin in 1867, Eisner was both a socialist and a pacifist. He worked as writer and editor in Munich and Nuremberg, and in 1914 agitated against Germany becoming involved in the dispute between Austria and Serbia. In 1918 he was briefly imprisoned for being a leader of one of the strikes which were beginning to cripple the German war effort. As chaos gradually replaced order within Germany, following the failure of the 'Kaiser's Battle' of early 1918, Eisner felt that Bavaria, whose capital Munich had been his home for many years, should break away from Germany. On the night of 7

[11]

8

7. Street fighting in Berlin – barricades

The struggle to maintain the rule of government against the tide of Bolshevist revolution, produced an uneasy liaison between the paramilitary Freikorps and the regular army. Here, in March 1919, they both man a street barricade as part of martial-law control of the city. A year later, however, Freikorps units tried to take over Berlin, a move that was defeated by a socialist general strike. As the Freikorps effort collapsed, a young man called Adolf Hitler arrived, hoping to co-ordinate a coup by the army in Bavaria with the coup in Berlin. He was too late.
German: Pub. unknown. 1919. Value B.

8. No meat

The picture, dated 2 May 1919, shows the carcass of a horse, killed during the Spartakist uprising in Munich, which is being cut up for food. The Socialists lost power before the year ended and it was here in Munich, at this time, that Adolf Hitler was serving with the 2nd Infantry Regiment. Later in the year he was sent by the army political department to spy on the German Workers' Party. This card is of particular note because it is produced from a photograph taken by Heinrich Hoffmann, who later became Hitler's close friend and photographer. It is interesting to speculate whether this is Hoffmann's first postcard and if, when it was published, he had yet met Hitler.
German: Pub. Heinrich Hoffmann, Munich. 1919. Value D.

9. Vienna

As Germany collapsed with the departure of the Kaiser and the spread of the socialist insurrections, so the Austro-Hungarian empire fell too. Vienna had been the capital of the empire which had been established by Emperor Franz Joseph in 1867, and it is his head that appears on the world's first postcard illustrated at 1. As civil disorder spread throughout Austria and Germany, both countries proclaimed themselves to be republics. There was much destruction and bloodshed for both countries in the turbulent years after the Armistice. This damage was done in a street riot.
Austrian. Pub. anon. *Circa* 1919. Value B.

10. F. Ebert, President of the German Republic

The flames of revolution had begun to spread across Germany before the Armistice of 11 November brought the First World War to an end. State government after state government collapsed, and finally, realising that his monarchy had lost control, the Kaiser abdicated. On 9 November he handed over power to the moderate socialists. They were led by Friedrich Ebert. That same day a German Republic was proclaimed. In order to maintain order Ebert sought the aid of the army, and with its help put down a number of workers' uprisings which earned him the hatred of the hard left. However, his actions demonstrated the central leadership that the National Assembly felt was essential to Germany's survival and on 11 February 1919 at Weimar, Ebert was elected President of the Republic. He died of appendicitis on 28 February 1925, and was succeeded by von Hindenburg. This is a mourning card issued in March 1925.
German: Pub. anon. Value B.

11. German National Assembly in Weimar 1919

This is an official postcard, issued to commemorate the opening of the Assembly at Weimar when Friedrich Ebert was elected as the first President of the new German Republic. Berlin, the traditional capital of Germany, had not been chosen to be the constitutional home of the new Republic because, just the month before, there had been a Spartakist uprising there and the city was considered to be unsafe. On the back of the card are three different commemorative stamps, each franked with a date stamp for 8 February 1919, three days before the election vote. The building shown is the old theatre in Weimar, where the assembly was held.
German: Pub. Reineck and Klein, Weimar. Designer Max Nehrling, Weimar. Value C.

9

10

11

KARL LIEBKNECHT

12

12. Karl Liebknecht

During the strikes that erupted across Germany from early in 1918, the extreme left socialist party, known as Spartakists, agitated for the overthrow of the Kaiser by armed revolution. Their leader was Karl Liebknecht. Liebknecht planned to engineer a left-wing coup in Berlin, but was pre-empted by the abdication of the Kaiser and the assumption of power by moderate socialist Friedrich Ebert on 9 November 1918. At first Ebert gave concessions to the Spartakists, but Liebknecht and his followers continued to foster discontent, and Ebert enlisted the help of the army to bring them under control. The army described its support of Ebert as a fight against 'Bolshevism' (so-called because in 1902 party conferences, Leninists were in the majority (Russian *Bolsheviki*)). Armed confrontations continued into 1919 (see captions 5, 6 and 7), by which time the Spartakists and others of the hard left had formed themselves into a Communist Party, complete with Russian advisers. Early in January, during violent clashes between communists and Freikorps, over 1,000 people were killed in Berlin alone and Liebknecht was murdered. The German Communist Party thus lost any real chance of gaining power. This card was issued after the defeat of Nazi Germany, on the Party Day of the German Communist Party, 19 April 1946, to commemorate the 25th anniversary of Liebknecht's death. It is franked on the back by SPD (socialist) and KPD (communist) cancellations. It shows Liebknecht speaking in Berlin's *Tiergarten* in December 1918.

German: Pub. KPD. Value B.

[13]

Ruhe und Ordnung wollen wir!

13

Tor auf nach Deutschland!

14

Bürgerbräukeller München   Pächter: Xaver Heilmannseder

15

Und Ihr habt doch gesiegt!

16

UND IHR HABT DOCH GESIEGT!

17

18

13. 'Ruhe und Ordnung'

The caption reads, 'We want rule and order'. The armed internal struggles which began in Germany before the First World War had ended, were symptoms of the larger conflict between the ideologies of extreme left, centre socialists and extreme right. Each was struggling to fill the gap created by the collapse of the monarchy. Between these three fires were the ordinary people, caught in much the same way as those in Northern Ireland are today between Loyalists, British Army and Republicans. This card was issued by the citizens of the 20th District of Munich in 1920. It is a plea for peace and quiet. Such conditions were a long way off.
German: Pub. Meisenbach Riffarth & Co., Munich, 1920. Value D.

14. 'Tor auf nach Deutschland!'

Open the door to Germany! Issued early in 1921, this card is a typical example of the pictorial propaganda issued by the various political groups jockeying for power and membership. In January the Allies had announced that Germany was expected to pay, as war reparations, the huge sum of 216 billion gold marks. Patriotic organisations – including the *Volksbund der Deutschen* that issued this card – held protest meetings to which thousands flocked.

Hitler was quick to hold his own NSDAP meetings to build his policy of undermining the Versailles Treaty. In June and July 1921 many citizens' militias were disbanded, as well as the Oberland Free Corps, and Hitler, who had taken full control of the Nazi Party on 3 August, found among their dispirited members many recruits for his newly formed SA.
German: Pub. Volksbund der Deutschen, 1921. Value D.

15. Burgerbraukeller, Munich

When Adolf Hitler first went as an army agent to spy on the German Workers' Party, their activities made little impression upon him, but at a second meeting held in the small Sterneckerbrau beer cellar, he suddenly realised that the fledgling organisation could provide him with the means to power. At this early stage, 12 September 1919, his activities, although driven by self-interest, were still covert actions on behalf of the army. Small cafés and beer cellars were convenient places to meet, ostensibly to have a beer with a few friends, and many of the buildings owned by the breweries could accommodate large crowds if the need arose. The consumption of liberal quantities of alcohol did much to encourage the enthusiasm of the gatherings. The Burgerbraukeller, which could hold up to 3,000 people, was designated an 'historic room' in the development of the NSDAP following its use as Hitler's command post during the abortive Munich *putsch* of 8/9 November 1923. It was also the scene of his first public meeting after his release from the imprisonment he had received as punishment for the attempted putsch. A less pleasant memory for Hitler would have been the bomb that was exploded there with the intention of killing him on 8 November 1939 and which killed Eva Braun's father. Of the principal cellars used by the Nazis, only the Hofbrauhaus in Munich is still in use today in anything like its original form. This card was probably published shortly after Hitler became Chancellor in 1933.
German: Pub. Preiss & Co., Munich. Value C.

16. 'Und Ihr habt doch gesiegt!'

When Hitler and Ludendorff marched into the centre of Munich at the head of some 3,000 NSDAP followers on the morning of 9 November 1923, they imagined it to be the beginning of a National Socialist revolution. It was not to be. They were fired upon by the police, and the marchers scattered in all directions. Hitler fell when Scheubner-Richter, with whom he had linked arms, was shot dead. Goering, too, was injured. Ludendorff, however, kept on marching until he reached the open vaulted arches of the *Feldherrnhalle*, erected in honour of great military heroes. The number of National Socialists killed varies from account to account. This card shows fourteen. Scheubner-Richter is in the second row up, third from the left.
German: Pub. Hoffmann, No. 1923. Value B.

17. 'Und Ihr habt doch gesiegt!'

Here are sixteen martyrs who were killed in the Munich putsch on 9 November 1923. The previous picture shows only fourteen. The extra names are F. Allfarth and W. Ehrlich and this list is presumably the 'official' NSDAP one, because the card shows the names as inscribed on the memorial which was erected at the Feldherrnhalle after the Nazis came to power.
German: Pub. Hoffmann. No. 671. Value B.

18. The Feldherrnhalle

In later years, after Hitler assumed absolute power over Germany, the scene of the shooting during the November 1923 putsch became hallowed ground. A memorial to the fallen was erected and given a permanent attendant guard. Each 9 November a remembrance ceremony and parade were held. This drawing, done in 1940 by Paul Hermann, shows that annual event.
German: Pub. Heinrich Hoffmann, for the House of German Art. Artist Paul Hermann. No. HDK 158. Value A.

19

München. Feldherrnhalle, Taubenfütterung

Front-Heil!

10. Reichsfrontsoldatentag des „Stahlhelm" (Bund der
deutschen Frontsoldaten) 1. u. 2. Juni 1929 in München

21

STAHLHELM

REICHSFRONT-
SOLDATENTAG
19 28
STAHLHELM HAMBURG

HAMBURG

20

ARRÊTEZ-VOUS !   I   HALT !
HALT !   ZATRZYMAĆ SIĘ !

22

L'EXTRÊME ONCTION   2   LETZTE OELUNG
EXTREME UNCTION   OSTATNIE NAMASZCZENIE

23

L'APPEL   3   APPEL
ROLL CALL   APEL

24

[16]

LE SOLDAT INCONNU   4   DER UNBEKANNTE SOLDAT
THE UNKNOWN SOLDIER   NIEZNANY ŻOŁNIERZ

25

CROIX D'HONNEUR   5   DIE «EHRENKREUZE»
THE FIELD OF HONOUR   KRZYŻE ZASŁUGI

26

19. The Feldherrnhalle

Although this very sharp, real photo presents a clear picture of the Feldherrnhalle, and the Nazi flags look impressive, they have been drawn in on the negative in order to up-date an old photograph. Once the Nazis came to power, it was almost *de rigueur* to have a swastika in every picture offered for sale.

German: Pub. Lengauer, Munich. Value A.

20, 21. 'Stahlhelm' (Steel Helmet) (two cards)

These cards have been issued by local branches (Hamburg and Munich) of the national German ex-soldier's organisation known as the Steel Helmet, which was formed after the Armistice. In 1920 the organisation supported the nationalistic ideas of the anti-communist movement and in 1929 Hitler publicly sided with the Stahlhelm in opposing the American 'Young Plan' proposal for the payment of German war reparations. When Hitler became Chancellor in 1933 thousands of Stahlhelm members marched in celebration under the Brandenburg Gate in Berlin, side by side with the SA and the SS. In 1937 the Prince of Wales, as Patron of the Royal British Legion, suggested that the Legion should visit Germany to 'stretch forth the hand of friendship' and the Stahlhelm joined other German ex-service organisations in welcoming the idea. The Stahlhelm lapel badge is a small German pattern steel helmet, similar in concept to the British pattern helmet badge of the MOTHs (Memorable Order of Tin Hats). Field Marshal Kesselring served as Chairman of the Stahlhelm after the Second World War.

German: Each card pub. for Stahlhelm. 1928/1929. Value C.

Colour illustration on page 73.

The ten striking designs which follow are from a set of twelve issued under the general title of *Vox Mortuum* meaning The Voice of the Dead. The appalling casualties suffered by both sides during the First World War produced a violent anti-war feeling among the European nations. The most extreme symptom of that feeling might, to some observers, be the appeasement policies of British Prime Minister Neville Chamberlain during the 1930s. Even at the beginning of the First World War the socialist and trade-union movements in Britain, France and Germany, were reluctant participants in the struggle. Today they tend to be in the forefront of the campaign against nuclear weapons and now, as then, they find support in women's movements. The *Vox Mortuum* campaign was sponsored by the World Union of Women for International Concord based in Geneva. The unique dilemma of the woman's position is chillingly captured by The Death Notice. Patriotism, and a desire to maintain a way of life, places insufferable pressures upon a wife and mother to send her men to war. 'Better red than dead' was a popular phrase of the peace-mongers during the communist scare period of the 1950s. However, as Adolf Hitler and his Nazi Party grew stronger, the 'peace-people' sensed a move towards another war and mobilised their propaganda forces to oppose it by opposing Hitler.

Swiss: Pub. The International Association of Propaganda by Picture. Artist B. Nowak-Varsovie. Each card Value C.

22. Halt!

23. Extreme Unction

24. Roll Call

25. The Unknown Soldier

26. The Field of Honour

LA LETTRE
THE DEATH-NOTICE   6   DIE TODESNACHRICHT
OSTATNI LIST

27

DAS WAISENKIND
SIEROTKA

L'ORPHELINE
THE ORPHAN

28

MALÉDICTION!
MALÉDICTION!   8   TRAUER UND FLUCH
PRZEKLEŃSTWO

29

DIE HAUPTUNTERSCHRIFT
NAJWAŻNIEJSZY PODPIS   9   LA PRINCIPALE SIGNATURE
THE PRINCIPAL SIGNATURE

30

27. The Death Notice

28. The Orphan

29. Malediction

30. The Principal Signature

31. SOS

32. Open Your Hearts

33. 'Nur das können wir!'

The only thing we know! Obviously it is how to shout!
There were plenty of people in Germany who did not
support the growing might of the Nazi Party, but as they
had from very early days at their political meetings, the
NSDAP used force to silence their opponents. That such
a card as this could survive the period of Nazi rule from
1933 to 1945, is extraordinary. The odds that the publisher
escaped without personal injury are very short indeed. An
extremely rare card.
German: Pub. Richard Kuter, Berlin. Value D.

S.O.S. (DÉSARMEMENT OU DÉSASTRE)   II   S.O.S. (ABRÜSTUNG ODER UNTERGANG)
S.O.S. (DISARMAMENT OR DISASTER)   S.O.S. (DOZBROJENIE LUB WAR)

31

OUVREZ VOS CŒURS   12   ŒFFNET EURE HERZEN!
OPEN YOUR HEARTS   OTWORZCIE SERCA!

32

33

BY GYULA ZILZER

FASCISM·MEANS WAR!
FASCHISMUS IST KRIEG!
LE FASCISME - C'EST LA GUERRE!
EL FASCISMO - ESTA LA GUERRA!

34

34. Fascism means war!

Those who strove to ensure peace had early warnings of the inevitable result of the rejuvenation of a country via totalitarian authority. In Italy in 1919, Mussolini had founded the Fascist movement, and through virulent propaganda, emotive speeches, extravagant parades and rallies, had mobilised the country behind him. He built up the armed forces and in 1935 began a series of adventures seeking to enhance Italy's international standing through military conquest. His first victory was in Ethiopia. Hitler was clearly going to follow the same path and he made no secret of his admiration for Il Duce. To those who recognised the danger signals, it was important to bring the United States into the world arena as anti-Fascist, since the intervention of the USA had had such a dramatic influence upon the ending of the First World War and the form of the peace that had followed it. The USA, however, in reaction to the war, was flirting with isolationist policies. This card was part of a campaign to open American eyes to the dangers of isolationism. It was published in Paris and distributed in the USA.

French: Pub. Edition du Carrefour, Paris. Artist Gyula Zilzer. Value B.

35

36

37

Reichskanzler Adolf Hitler vor seinem

Wohnhaus in Berchtesgaden

38

39

35, 36. War against war (two cards)

The peace message of these cards, issued in the mid-1920s, is not directed specifically against the Nazis, but rather against the capitalists. Indeed one card, referring to war, has the caption 'Do it yourself Boss'! Nevertheless the publishers, the International Federation of Trade Unions, would view any authoritarian regime as anti-worker and once Hitler was in power in Germany in 1933 he acted immediately to destroy the power of the trade unions.

Dutch: Pub. International Federation of Trade Unions. Value C.

EWIGE WACHT FÜR
SÜDTIROL

40

41

37. Hitler's house at Obersalzberg

Early on in his political career Hitler had felt the need for a place to hide, somewhere where he could relax with friends or simply be alone. The majesty of the Alps which bordered his native Austria, fitted the scale of his own ambitions, and their soaring peaks matched the grandeur of Wagner's music which he loved so much. As his fame grew so the simple house halfway up the Kehlstein mountain at Upper Salzberg lost its solitude, but he never tired of it.

German: Pub. anon. *circa* 1930. Value C.

38. Reich Chancellor Adolf Hitler in front of his house at Berchtesgaden

Berchtesgaden is a town lying on the northern side of the Alps in south-east Bavaria, close to Salzburg and the Austro-German border. It had been used as a resort by the Bavarian monarchy and Hitler chose it as a retreat in the early 1920s. At first he stayed in the Pension Moritz, using the assumed name of Herr Wolf, but in 1928 found a place to himself – the Haus Wachenfeld (later completely rebuilt and renamed the Berghof — 'Mountain House'), at Obersalzberg, 1,500 ft (457 m) above Berchtesgaden. The house was originally a simple, typically Bavarian structure, with a wooden verandah, which Hitler used as his headquarters, frequently inviting top Nazis to visit him there. He was fond of walking over the mountain slopes and often wore *Lederhosen* (leather shorts).

Many propaganda pictures show Hitler in his leather shorts, gazing thoughtfully out across the mountains.

German: Pub. Photo-Pringstl, Berchtesgaden. Posted 13 September 1933. Value D.

39. The Führer having a quiet break in the mountains

This picture was probably taken in the early 1930s, but the card was posted on 15 August 1943 and the Führer probably needed a break then. The German armies had been driven out of North Africa, the Allies were in control of Sicily and poised to invade Italy and the Russian summer offensive was in full swing.

German: Pub. Hoffmann. No. 676. Value B.

40. Everlasting vigil for South Tyrol

South Tyrol was, before the First World War, a province of Austria lying within the Alps between Bavaria and Italy, which was ceded to Italy in 1919. Both Hitler and Mussolini had designs on it. When Hitler was in prison in 1924, following the failure of the Munich putsch, Goering attempted to borrow 2 million lire from Mussolini to help Hitler's cause. In return, Goering offered the public support of the Nazi Party for Mussolini's claim on the Tyrol. Nothing came of the offer. The pressure from neighbours led to the formation of private Tirolese political armies for self-defence, of which the major ones were the *Schutzbund*, organised by the Social Democrats, and the *Heimwehr* of the Christian Socialists. This card, issued by the Friends of the Heimwehr, was probably sold as a fund raiser.

Tirolean: Pub. Tirolean Homeland League, Innsbruck. Early 1930. Value D.

Colour illustration on page 73.

41. A Room in Hitler's house

In 1928 Hitler rented this small, two-storey house in Berchtesgaden called Haus Wachenfeld. It was typically Bavarian, with heavy wooden furniture and hunting trophies adorning the walls. His monthly rent was about £10. In 1929, probably using the money earned from his book *Mein Kampf*, he bought the building outright. Progressively he enlarged and improved the house and, once he became Chancellor in 1933, major alterations were made to accord with his new importance.

German: Pub. Hoffmann. No. 470. Value B.

[21]

42

Der Führer mit R. Heß auf Haus Wachenfeld.

43

Eine originelle Begegnung

44

45

Auch ich wünsche Dir alles Gute, mein FÜHRER!

46

47

48

45. Horst Wessel

As the Nazi movement continued to grow stronger, and its leader reached out towards the Chancellorship, the need for ever more dramatic rallies and propaganda events stretched even Goebbels' imagination. Wessel, a 21-year-old law student, was an enthusiastic Brownshirt and, like Hess, participated in many street battles against the Communists. Early in 1930 he was shot by a Red gang and Goebbels made immediate use of his death by having sung at a mass Nazi rally a song 'Die Fahne Hoch' (Raise High the Flag) that Wessel had composed. The funeral march turned into a pitched battle between Nazis and Communists and the song became a battle hymn that was then regularly used by the Nazis and called the 'Horst Wessel Lied' (song) This picture purports to show Wessel at a 1929 Nuremberg Rally.

German: Pub. Hoffmann. No. 405. Value D.

42. Hitler's house

This is a room in the same building as mentioned in the previous picture (41). The house, on the lower slopes of the Kehlstein mountain in Berchtesgaden, attracted great attention, and so many sightseers came that the surroundings eventually became a restricted area. Major alterations after 1933 were accompanied by the changing of the name of the house to Berghof (Mountain House). Eva Braun had her own rooms in the building and later other major Nazi figures, such as Martin Bormann and Goering, built houses nearby.

German: Pub. Hoffmann. No. 422. Value B.

43. The Führer with Rudolph Hess

By an odd coincidence, Hess served in the same infantry regiment as Adolf Hitler during the First World War, though later he qualified as a pilot. After the Armistice he joined the right-wing Freikorps and took part in street battles against the Communists. An early member of the Nazi Party, he became very close to Hitler and voluntarily joined him in prison after the failure of the Munich putsch. There, and later, he helped Hitler in the writing of *Mein Kampf*. They are seen here in the Berghof (Haus Wachenfeld) overlooking the Unterberg.

German: Pub. Hoffmann. No. 217. Value B.

44. A strange encounter

The three cyclists are chimney sweeps and the one on the right is holding the traditional top hat, which is still worn on the Continent today. In the mid-1920s, following his release from prison, Hitler drove around the countryside with a small group of associates, planning his return to public life. One of the group was the photographer Hoffmann. It is quite possible that the Führer's car met these sweeps on one such drive and Hoffmann arranged the picture as an omen of good luck. Such sweeps with bicycles can still be seen in Germany today.

German: Pub. Hoffmann. No. 314. Value C.

46. Good wishes to you my Führer

Hitler seemed genuinely fond of children, though he saw them *en masse* as Germany's future. Through organisations like the Hitler Youth and the German Students' Bund he organised their development and moulded their attitudes towards total commitment to Nazi ideas. Here he is doing what politicians still do today — using a child as a vote catcher.

German: Pub. Hoffmann. Value B.

47. An early Nazi group

This is an early photo, probably produced as a postcard for one of those pictured in it. The date is the mid- to late-1920s. The skilful use of uniform and pageant, and the controlled award of badges as symbols of merit, were major contributors to the popularity of the Nazi movement. A sense of belonging to something substantial and exciting accompanied the issue of uniform and title. This group display a varied selection of uniforms, including a splendid ceremonial head-dress, which can just be made out at the left rear. Perhaps this is a group of new Nazi recruits.

German: Pub. anon. Value B.

48. Hitler & Co.

Adolf Hitler certainly knew how to produce an impressive line-up. This gathering at a party meeting in Nuremberg has a remarkable consistency in dress. There were so many individualistic people in the Nazi hierarchy that the apparently simple problem of getting them to wear the same uniform, must have assumed gigantic proportions. Hitler was not flamboyant in his turn-out and the evidence of the effect of his force of will on the others is very clear. Among those in the line-up are left to right Todt, Goebbels, Lutze, Hitler, Hess and Streicher.

German: Pub. Hoffmann. No. P.66. *Circa* 1932. Value C.

49

50

51

52

53

54

[24]

49. Hitler and Co.

Hitler with a group of lesser mortals in Nuremberg. 'Germany Day' rallies had been held in Nuremberg since the early 1920s and they were timed to coincide with the anniversary of von Moltke's 1870 victory over the French at Sedan, when Napoleon III was taken prisoner. Ironically, the failure of Germany's 'Schlieffen Plan' to overcome France and Russia in 1914, was blamed upon the alterations made to the plan by the then Chief of Staff – von Moltke's nephew.

German: Pub. Hoffmann. No. P.2. Value B.

50. 'Deutschland erwache' (Germany awake)

After the failure of his Munich putsch in November 1923, Hitler was jailed. During his confinement he began to write *Mein Kampf* and reflected upon how he could gain power in Germany. He resolved that everything he did would always have the cloak of legality, and part of that plan was to fight elections, both for regional and national representation. The Nazi Party had 150,000 members by 1928, two years after Hitler's release from prison, and two years after that polled 6.5 million votes in the national elections for seats in the *Reichstag*. Early in 1932 Hitler contested the Presidential elections against Hindenburg and lost narrowly, but on 31 July 1932 the Nazi Party became the largest group in the Reichstag, by winning· 230 seats in the national election and polling over 13,700,000 votes. This card shows a Brownshirt SA team electioneering on behalf of Hitler and the Nazis. The place is Bad Oeynhausen, but the actual year is uncertain. It is plainly 1932 or earlier because, once the Nazis had gained control, there was no further need for elections. The large swastika on wheels reads 'Germany Awake. Vote'. The word 'swastika', of Sanskrit origin, means 'all is all', and had been used by Teutonic Knights. The origins of the sign are certainly pre-Christian and, until the Nazis adopted it in 1920, it had been universally regarded as a good luck symbol.

German: Pub. N. Rybak, Bad Oeynhausen. *Circa* 1930. Value C.

51. Hitler & Co.

The Nazi philosophy covered every aspect of German life. Films, books and even paintings had to be 'approved'. The workers, the children and the women were organised in sectarian groups with their own codes, hierarchies and uniforms. Here, Hitler is acknowledging the plaudits of the audience at a gathering of the National Socialist Women's Organisation, whose leader, Frau Scholtz-Klink, is sitting to his right. Goebbels can be seen to Hitler's left. In the days before Hitler became Chancellor, he took every opportunity to appear in public in order to promote and to emphasise his party's philosophies.

German: Pub. Hoffmann. No. 710. Value B.

52. 'Obersalzberg Besuch' (Obersalzberg visit)

Obersalzberg is synonymous with Berchtesgaden. The latter word means 'mountain garden' but so strongly is it associated with the Hitler period, that today Bavarians deliberately refer to the area as Obersalzberg. Visitors flocked to see Hitler's home, first named 'Haus Wachenfeld' and later 'Berghof'. At the peak, during the 1930s, some 5,000 visitors a day toiled up the side of the Kehlstein mountain and Martin Bormann converted a nearby local hotel, the 'Platterhof', into a 'National Hotel' to provide accommodation. That hotel, now named the 'General Walker' is currently an American Forces rest centre.

German: Pub. Hoffmann. No. 229. Value B.

53. 'Der Freund der Arbeiter' (The worker's friend)

Hitler was an excellent propagandist and this card is a fine example of Nazi teamwork. Hoffmann, the photographer, has caught Hitler at such an angle that he appears to be taller than his audience, thus suggesting leadership. There. is no doubting that the audience is listening to what Hitler is saying and their rapt attention has been captured in detail by the camera. Brotherly identification with the workers is emphasised by the absence of uniform, and the use of a postcard as a vehicle for the picture is ideal, since the workers used cards in preference to writing letters. During the late 1920s and early 1930s, Germany suffered from massive unemployment which, once in power, Hitler began to solve by creating a national labour force (*Arbeitsdienst*). They were put to work on the new autobahns.

German: Pub. Hoffmann. No. 233. Value B.

54. 'München, Braunes Haus'

This large square, known as the 'Koenig's Platz', was originally an open grassy space. Hitler had it paved in order to hold parades there. The building on the left, the Brown House, was opened as NSDAP Party HQ on 1 January 1931. On the ground floor was a small refreshment room and above were the offices of Goebbels, Hess and other senior Nazis. Hitler's own office overlooked the Platz and contained a portrait of Frederick the Great and a bust of Mussolini. The name Brown House comes from the SA movement, whose HQ was on the first floor, and whose uniforms were brown.

German: Pub. August Lengauer. Munich. *Circa* 1932. Value C.

Triumph of the Will 1933-1936

In the years of struggle leading up to his appointment as Chancellor on 30 January 1933, Hitler perfected the methods of mass persuasion. He practised and polished his own techniques of oratory, carefully rehearsing his gestures and his intonations. This same attention to detail he demanded of those around him and, within a few hours of his assuming the Chancellorship, began assembling the jig-saw elements of mass coercion. Once in power Hitler was determined to stay there. But there was much to be done. The industrialists and the army thought that he was their puppet, and the Reichstag and the Reich President Hindenburg still stood in the way of supreme power.

Very quickly, Hermann Goering, Prussian Minister of the Interior, began replacing government officials at all levels with Nazi Party members. Policeman were dismissed and SA men took their places. In April Goering set up the *Gestapo* (secret police) and charged them with the location and arrest of all political suspects. It was, in effect, the end of the judiciary, since the Gestapo went on to assume even the responsibility of judgment and punishment.

The SA at this time numbered some 3 million men, and could thus directly confront the regular army, the *Reichswehr*, which made the latter, theoretically limited to a maximum strength of 100,000, very nervous. However the SA was composed largely of layabouts and fugitives from unemployment, without a firm code of discipline or experienced military leaders. The only base from which Hitler could develop military might was the Reichswehr. Therefore, just a few days after his appointment, he won over senior officers to his cause by promising them

that the Reichswehr would be Germany's only armed organisation.

Nevertheless Hitler still did not control the Reichstag or have the support of all the State governments. He was therefore unable to make changes to the constitution of the Republic. What he now needed was a national election in which the Nazis obtained a landslide victory. Using the emergency powers of the constitution, he restricted political meetings and assumed control over the Press. Goebbels began to swamp the media with Nazi propaganda and the SA took command of the streets.

Just a week before the 5 March election, the Reichstag building was burned down. Hitler and the Nazis frenetically blamed the Communists for starting the fire and persuaded von Hindenburg that the safety of the State was threatened. The old President signed an emergency decree, which in effect suppressed all civil liberties. But the election results were disappointing. The Nazis did not poll enough votes to give them the two-thirds majority which was needed in the Reichstag in order for them to make changes to the constitution.

Undeterred, the Hitler and Goebbels propaganda machine worked hard at emphasising the communist threat, and one month later the new Reichstag voted on a bill to give Hitler's government total authority for four years to put down the 'red peril'. The propaganda worked, and Hitler got his two-thirds majority. It was in effect the end of the Weimar Republic and the end of parliamentary rule in Germany.

By June, trade unions had been abolished and in

July, Germany was declared a one-party state. Hitler now had 'legal' dictatorial control over the nation and had no further need of the unruly SA as his major force. He also had to fulfil his promise to the Reichswehr, and to do that he had to destroy the power of the SA. On 30 June 1934, under plans drawn up by Heinrich Himmler, 150 SA leaders were executed by the SS. Over a three-day period some 1000 people were killed. When von Hindenburg died on 1 August Hitler promoted himself to President and the Reichswehr swore allegiance to him. He was supreme dictator. It had taken just twenty months from his appointment as Chancellor.

Adolf Hitler did not have everyone's support, but he was skilful and ruthless enough to get his own way. As far as the general public was concerned he appeared to be a Saviour. The Nazis were identified with Germany, and Germany with Hitler, and Hitler with the people – 'one people, one country, one leader'. The whole effect was promoted via a myriad of organised specialist interests for youth, for girls, for mothers and children, for workers, apparently for all the poorer 'German' elements of the nation. Emotional and effective appeals for sectarian and national loyalty, bolstered by dramatic parades, were regular party activities.

Much of the splendid pageantry and spectacle that the Nazis used to sway their massive audiences was copied from Mussolini's Fascists, but Hitler, unlike Mussolini, gathered around him a team of competent aides, who extended and improved upon Il Duce's innovations. Great use was made of 'Special Days', such as 'Reich Party Day', or 'Workers' and 'Farmers' Day' in order to encourage community marching and singing with an inevitable Nazi speech at the end. It was superb showmanship with the Führer travelling frenetically from one event to another. The single most important rally was the *Reichsparteitag* at Nuremberg.

Hitler's first experience of a major nationalist rally had been on the *Deutscher Tag* (German Day) held in Nuremberg in September 1923, and when he began to rebuild the party after his release from Landsberg prison, he decided that all NSDAP mass rallies would be held in Nuremberg. They began in 1927 with the 'Day of Awakening', followed two years later by the 'Party Day of Consolidation'. There they stopped. Hitler was too involved in the tense and complicated struggle for power, but when he became Chancellor in 1933 they began again. Hitler decreed Nuremberg to be the *Stadt der Reichsparteitag* (the Party Day city). The 1933 name, 'Party Day of Victory' was chosen by Rudolf Hess to celebrate Hitler's appointment as Chancellor and the rally lasted from 1 to 7

September, a period which promised to offer the best weather. All future rallies were held in early September in the hope of good conditions, and fine weather thereafter became known as 'Führer weather'.

The rallies were spectacular, emotional events, stage-managed in every detail. To be there was to experience a feeling akin to religious fervour. To take part was to participate in an altar call, to re-commit oneself to the party. In 1934 came 'Triumph of the Will'. On the second evening Goering placed 130 *Luftwaffe* searchlights around the Zeppelin Field and 200,000 people, with a flag between every 10 of them, came to hear their Führer speak. The 'Party Day of Freedom' followed in 1935 and the 'Party Day of Honour' in 1936.

So important a place did the Reichsparteitag events hold in the NSDAP calendar, that Albert Speer was commissioned by Hitler to design a massive complex in which they could be staged. Work began in 1935, and the plans included parade areas such as the Zeppelin Field (where Count von Zeppelin landed his airships in 1909), for political and armed forces events, plus, nearby, the Luitpold arena for the SA, the SS and other NSDAP units. There was also a Congress Hall, a Great Road and other ambitious projects. Much of the design was never finished, but the Zeppelin and Luitpold arenas were used. Today, much of the area is a housing estate, though the concrete shell of the Congress Hall and the regular lines of the Zeppelin Field tribune are plain to see.

The core of Hitler's plan to unite the German nation was, however, negative, and based upon fear, hate and envy. He reasoned that great leaders united their followers by giving them a clear and simple cause. Hitler chose a scapegoat – the Jews. He blamed them for everything bad that had happened to Germany and the NSDAP cause became the elimination of the Jew from the land.

As early as 1919, in point number four of the twenty-five-point party programme which he wrote for the new NSDAP, Hitler professed that 'no Jew can be a member of the nation', and as the Nazis gained increasing power, so overt actions against Jewish individuals and businesses became more violent. Two months after Hitler's appointment as Chancellor, a nationwide boycott of Jewish shops, monitored by uniformed SA men, was introduced. By 1935 over a quarter of a million Jews had left the country voluntarily, fearing for their lives. They were wise to go. On 15 September that year the 'Nuremberg Blood Laws' were enacted. They 'legalised' point number four. Jews were no longer citizens of Germany.

Hitler had other hates. Nazi treatment of the

Communists lagged very little behind that of the Jews, and other minority groups stood in line as targets – as did the Church. But the mixture of hate, drama, spectacle, charismatic leadership and growing prosperity fuelled by a war-like economy, was a heady one. Most people approved of what they chose to see and the nation briskly followed its Führer forward to 1936 when Germany planned to demonstrate the superiority of the Aryan race to the world at the Berlin Olympics.

55

56

57

58

59

55. Chancellor Adolf Hitler and President Hindenburg

Following the July elections in 1932, the Nazis held more seats in the Reichstag than any other party, although power still remained with Chancellor von Papen. When the Nazis contrived to outvote Papen, the latter dissolved the chamber and called for new elections in November. However, Papen did not gain any advantage from his action and was forced to resign. On 17 November 1932, Hindenburg offered the Chancellorship to Hitler, who turned it down because the President would not grant him full powers. Reichswehr General Kurt von Schleicher took office as Chancellor in December, but was unable to obtain co-operation from the Nazis and the Communists to form a government, and so he too asked the President if elections could again be held. Former Chancellor von Papen, meanwhile, had obtained behind the scenes guarantees of co-operation from the Nazis and the Nationalists, and he persuaded Hindenburg to refuse Schleicher's request and to offer the Chancellorship once more to Hitler. This time, aware of a decline in the popularity of his Nazi Party, Hitler accepted, and on 30 January 1933 became Chancellor of a coalition government. It was the beginning of the end for democratic government in Germany. Hindenburg had only another year to live, and during that time Hitler took great pains to see that his public attitude towards the ageing President was deferential.
German: Pub. Hoffmann. No. 379. 1933. Value B.

56. Hitler & Co.

In the centre of the marching column are Goering and Hitler. The date is 9 November 1933, just nine months after Hitler's appointment as Chancellor. The place is Munich. When the two men had marched together in that same city in 1923, ten years earlier to the day, they had been fired upon by the police. Goering had been wounded and had fled to Austria. Hitler had been searched out, tried and imprisoned. Now they were effectively the two most powerful men in Germany. It must have been an intoxicating experience for them.
German: Pub. Hoffmann. No. 192310. 1933. Value B.

57. Party Day 1933

Flags, banners and standards played important roles in Nazi rituals. The Romanesque NSDAP standards, which can be seen clearly here, were probably based upon a design drawn up by Hitler himself. As each new local branch or unit of SA or SS was formed, its flag was consecrated in some special ceremony. Ceremonies performed on the main party days in Nuremberg would involve touching the new standards with the 'Blood Flag', the flag that had been carried during the putsch in 1923.
German: Pub. Hoffmann. 1933. Value B.

58. Potsdam, 21 March 1933

Further proof that Hitler did hold genuine respect for von Hindenburg was his decision to open his new, and first, Reichstag, in Potsdam. To Prussian military tradition it was what Aldershot is to the British Army. Frederick the Great is buried there. This card commemorates the opening of the Reichstag with Hitler as Chancellor and Hindenburg as President. From a solemn beginning, when Hindenburg laid a wreath on Frederick the Great's tomb, the assembly went on to hear a speech from the new Chancellor that was acclaimed by the Nazi delegates singing the 'Horst Wessel song'. The card was published by the family firm of Hanfstaengl, whose members had been enthusiastic supporters of Hitler since 1922.
German: Artist Carl Langhorst. Pub. Hanfstaengl. No. 13347. 1933. Value C.

59. Deutschland, Deutschland über alles! 30 Jan. 1933

This official stationery postcard shows a small picture of the rejoicing marchers streaming through the Brandenburg Gate in Berlin on the night of 30 January 1933, the day that Hitler became Chancellor. Torchlight processions went on for many hours, watched by Hitler and Hindenburg. There were many marching songs that echoed across the city from the Tiergarten to the President's palace and among them were 'Deutschland' and 'Horst Wessel'. This card was posted on 3 February 1934 and the message (in German) which it carried gives a perfect cameo of life in Germany during the early years of Nazi rule – and shows that some Germans, at least, were pleased with things.

Translation: 'Invitation!'

> Dear Bartelmann,
> I have just read in the 'V.B.' [i.e., 'Volkischer Beobachter' newspaper] that your [rowing] eight has been admitted for the Olympic trials. Surely George Bartelmann is the coach and I wish you the best of luck, that is to say, naturally, 'break a leg'! So, dear old 'Bartelboy', now there'll be sound sporting participation again, eh? Doesn't our new Germany do your heart good?
> How is the 'Bartelwife', alias 'Bartelmam' and the 'Bartelson'? Hopefully all is well with you, as can by and large be said of us too. I am an Office Manager with the PO and my two boys are SA [i.e., Sturmabteilung] men with the 48th motorised squadron; Hans is squadron adjutant and the younger Hermann is paymaster, for which his job as a bank employee suits him well.
> The entire Bepler household awaits a visit from the South German Bartelmanns again in Wetzlar, to be able to welcome them and closes in that vein. Heil Hitler!
> Hermann Bepler.

The underlining has been added by the authors.
German: Pub. German Post Office. 1933. Value B.
Colour illustration on page 73.

60

61

62

63

64

65

60. Nuremberg 1933

The first party rally had been held in January 1923, the year of the ill-fated putsch. Here, ten years later, was the 5th rally, the first that Hitler attended as Chancellor. Suitably named 'The Party Day of Victory', it lasted from 1 to 7 September, with parades involving over 150,000 uniformed men. During the ceremonies the Blood Flag was paraded and new standards consecrated. Hitler decreed that in future all central party rallies would be held in Nuremberg and ordered that special arenas should be constructed. On the second day he gave his personal SS bodyguard unit a new name: 'SS Leibstandarte Adolf Hitler'. The card, in effect, says 'One people – strong nation'.

German: Pub. Franz Eher on behalf of the NSDAP. 1933. Official rally card. Value D.

Colour illustration on page 73.

61. 'Reichsparteitag'. Nuremberg 1934

In August 1934 President von Hindenburg died. Thus Adolf Hitler came to Nuremberg in September 1934 as Commander-in-Chief of the armed forces, Chancellor and complete dictator of Germany. The parade of participants took more than five hours to pass through the town and when Hitler spoke on the Zeppelin Field there were over 400,000 people there to hear him. The rally, which ran from 5 to 10 September, was filmed by Leni Riefenstahl, who named her work 'Triumph of the Will', and this title was retrospectively attached to the rally itself. So spectacular were the parades, and so excellent the footage, that no other rallies were filmed, and even today there is considerable demand for video-tape versions of the work. The design shown here formed the basis of the official rally badge.

German: Artist Richard Klein. Pub. Franz Eher on behalf of the NSDAP. 1934 Official rally card. Value D.

62. 'Reichspartietag'. Nuremberg, 5–10 September 1934

This design by Seigmar von Suchodolski depicts an SA man. The SA had lost its leader, Röhm, in the 'Night of the Long Knives' purge in July 1934. His replacement, Victor Lutze, unlike Röhm, owed total allegience to Hitler, and was thus subordinate in every way to him. The SA declined in importance as the SS grew in influence. An innovation at this rally was the *Reichsarbeitsdienst* (Reich Workers) parade: 50,000 men carrying shovels marched and drilled.

German: Artist S. von Suchodolski. Pub. Franz Eher on behalf of the NSDAP. 1934. Official rally card. Value D.

Colour illustration on page 73.

63. Nuremberg 1935. German unity – German strength

This rally covered the period 10–16 September, and was named the 'Party Day of Freedom'. Hitler was having personal difficulties with a sore throat following a minor operation, and harboured fears that he might have cancer. Nevertheless he delivered a major speech on 11 September and from it, two days later, came the 'Nuremberg Blood Law', in which it was ruled that only those of, 'German or related' blood, could be citizens of the state, i.e. no Jews. Hitler had also been steadily increasing the size of his armed forces, the *Wehrmacht*, and during a display on the final day of the rally, German tanks and bombers were seen. The card design shows SA men.

German: Artist Mjolnir (Hans Schweitzer). Pub. Franz Eher on behalf of the NSDAP. 1935. Official rally card. Value D.

64. 'Reichsparteitag'. Nuremberg 1934

This official German post office card (the stamp is printed on the board) uses a poster design by Mjolnir, who had enthusiastically supported the Nazis from the beginning. One of his early posters had described Hitler as 'Germany's Last Hope'. This card carries a commemorative automatic cancellation, which was available in several of the special post offices established to serve the rally. The stamp shows the old castle at Nuremberg.

German: Artist Mjolnir (Hans Schweitzer). Pub. German Post Office. 1934. Value B.

65. National holiday 1934

On 23 March 1933 Adolf Hitler was given total power by the Reichstag to destroy 'the red peril'. He wasted no time in intensifying a process which had already begun and which was called *Gleichshaltung* (streamlining). Local officials at all levels of government and state administration were dismissed and replaced by Nazis. Soon, attention turned to the trade unions whose officials were attacked and beaten, prompting a formal complaint to the Chancellor from the Chairman of the Trade Union Congress. The traditional May Day celebrations took place under the title 'National Labour Day', with apparent Nazi approval, but twenty-four hours later the SA broke into left-wing trade union offices, arrested the officials and sent most of them to concentration camps. In June the Trade Union movement was dissolved and replaced by the German Labour Front. This official card celebrates May Day 1934, the first Labour Day of the Nazi régime.

German: Pub. German Post Office. 1934. Value B.

66

67

69

68

70

66. '1 Mai. Tag der Nationalen Arbeit'

The first day in May has traditionally been a time to celebrate the changing seasons, and in England in Tudor times it was a public holiday. The International Socialist Congress of 1889 named 1 May as 'International Labour Day', with a view to establishing it as a national holiday. In Europe, 1 May became associated with the trade unions and when Hitler disbanded the unions in 1933 he replaced them with the German Labour Front. This card celebrates 1 May 1935 the first 'Day of the German Labour Front'. German: Pub. NSDAP Munich. 1935. Value D.

67. Germany's disarmament and the armament of her neighbours

The Treaty of Versailles limited the German Army, the Reichswehr, to a maximum strength of 100,000 men. Hitler's professed aim was to negate the treaty's conditions and to recover for Germany her lost lands. That could not be done with an army of 100,000 and so a propaganda campaign justifying his progressive re-armament was needed. This card is part of that carefully co-ordinated campaign and was probably issued in 1935, the year that German compulsory military service was re-introduced.

[32]

71

72

Chancellorship was the vote to be taken in the Saar. On 13 January 1935, the people were to say 'Yes' or 'No' to re-joining Germany. A strong 'Yes' would encourage Britain and America to be tolerant towards Hitler's ambitions, and the full might of Nazi propaganda was aimed at encouraging the 'Yes' vote. This card, published in Saarbrücken, carries a compelling question – 'We died for you. Will you betray us?' (by voting 'No'). Obviously published before 13 January, this card has been date-stamped 13 January, 1935.
German: Pub. Hofer, Saarbrücken. *Circa* 1934. Value D.

69. 13 January, 1935
Further evidence of pressure placed on the Saar populace to vote as the countdown to 13 January, plebiscite day, continued. Hitler obtained his 'Yes' vote. With the urging of the Roman Catholic Church to encourage them, more than 90 per cent of the Saar people voted to join Germany.
German: Pub. Hofer, Saarbrucken. Value C.

70. The Nuremberg Stadium
The top picture shows the Rostrum of Honour, a stone structure 396 m (1,300 ft) long and 24 m (80 ft) high, built by Albert Speer for the 1934 party rally, and from which Hitler spoke. The lower view is towards the *Totenehrung*, the Memorial to the Dead, and the stadium, when completed in 1934, was the largest in the world. Today, nothing remains of the stadium, which was in the Luitpold arena, although there is a restored memorial there to German war-dead, based upon the old Totenehrung.
German: Pub. Riffelmacher. *Circa* 1935. Value B.

71. Hitler and Co.
The Führer is inspecting a parade of the *Arbeitsdienst*, the German Labour Corps, a State-organised force which was created by the Nazis to alleviate the massive unemployment prevalent during the Weimar régime. Experience gained in the formation, and use of the Corps, proved a great value when Hitler later mobilised the whole nation for war.
German: Pub. Hoffmann. No. 567. *Circa* 1935. Value B.

72. 'Deutschland ist Erwacht!' (Germany is awake)
On NSDAP banners and standards the rallying cry 'Germany Awake' was used with great effect to stir the emotions of audiences at party rallies. On 30 January 1933 Hitler became Chancellor of Germany, and achieved what he and his colleagues had been aiming at for so long. This card celebrates that appointment. 'Germany is (now) Awake'. The small pictures show, left to right, Chancellor Hitler, President Hindenburg and Franz Seldte, leader of the right-wing *Stahlhelm* (Steel Helmet) veterans' organisation. The Stahlhelm men had joined with the SA and SS in the torchlight parades through Berlin's Brandenburg Gate on the evening of Hitler's appointment and supplemented the SA and SS whenever brute force was needed.
German: Pub. E. Hennings. Berlin. Series 1, 1933. Value B.

On the back is printed the message 'The one-sided dis-armament of Germany seriously endangers her security as long as her neighbours do not disarm in a similar manner. The German people unanimously demand the same rights and the same security as other nations and claim an absolute equality of status with regard to this vital question.' In 1983 similar arguments were put forward by NATO to justify the installation of American Cruise missiles.
German: Pub. probably NSDAP. *Circa* 1935. Value D. Colour illustration on page 73.

68. 'Wir starben für Euch! Und Ihr wollt uns verraten?'
In Hitler's plan to recover Germany's territorial losses, was an initial dependence upon the sympathy of other European countries for German suffering as a result of the Versailles Treaty. He believed that in both Britain and America there would be high-level support, or at least 'blind eyes', for any breaches by Germany of the treaty's terms. However, the first real test of the old German territories' support of his

73

74

Die Saar ist frei! Saarbrücken, 13. Januar 1935.

75

Reichspräsident v. Hindenburg auf dem Totenbett.
† 2. VIII. 1934 in Neudeck

76

EINZUG DER BLUTFAHNE

77

78

[34]

73. Hitler and Co.

'The Olympic Games'. Hitler is here seen leading a column of dignitaries across the field within the Berlin Olympic Stadium in 1936. Oddly, the terraces behind the column are empty, so this may have been a rehearsal for the event, which was intended to demonstrate to the world the superiority of the 'Master Race'. The Nazis had learned very early on that detailed stage management was essential if the desired results were to be obtained from rallies and parades, and by 1936 they were masters of the art. The Olympic Stadium, now Headquarters of the British Forces in Berlin, was designed to seat 100,000 people and a radio station was built in order to broadcast German victories to the world.
German: Pub. Atlantic Photo, Berlin. Official Olympic card, No. 19. 1936. Value B.

74. Saar

Between his entry into politics and his appointment by Hindenburg, Hitler's aim had been to become Chancellor. Once in that position, he immediately began to place Nazis in all positions of authority, moving towards total assumption of power and dictatorship. One of his stated longer-term objectives, which had helped to rally the population behind him, was to recover for Germany those territories taken away from her by the Treaty of Versailles. This card shows a superbly staged rally of Hitler Youth during the Party Day period in September 1934. Part of carefully co-ordinated Nazi propaganda, this demonstration was designed to influence the outcome of the Saar voting, which was due just four months later.
German: Pub. Hoffmann. No. P.19. Value C.

75. The Saar is Free!

Saarbrucken, 13 January 1935. After Germany's defeat in the First World War, the Saar mining area was ceded to France as part of the war reparations that Germany was required to pay under the Treaty of Versailles, and from January 1920 was placed under a governing commission of the League of Nations. At the end of fifteen years, on 13 January 1935, a plebiscite was held in which the population of the Saar was able to choose between remaining under the control of the League of Nations, or becoming part of Germany. Following much Nazi propaganda and alleged intimidation at the polls, the area cast over 90 per cent of its votes for a return to Germany. The picture shows celebrations shortly after the poll result had been made known. The mass of flags carrying swastikas is clear evidence of the Nazi fever.
German: Pub. T. Klem. Saarbrücken. January 1935. Value C.

76. The Death of Hindenburg

This magnificent black-bordered card shows the President on his death bed lying in state. The old soldier had always preferred iron cots and the simple frame can be clearly seen. Hindenburg had been under continual strain as Germany's father figure for many years, and although he did not get on with Hitler on a personal basis, he recognised that at last Germany had a strong leader. Perhaps it was a combination of relief at the lifting of some of the burdens of state from his shoulders, and reaction to such bloody Nazi techniques as the 'Night of the Long Knives', that brought on a rapid deterioration in his health. He died at 9 a.m. on 2 August 1934 at his estate in Neudeck in East Prussia. Hitler had visited him the day before, and seeing that the President's death was imminent, flew back to Berlin. Just three hours after Hindenburg died Hitler declared himself 'Führer' and Reich Chancellor. That same day, all the armed forces swore a personal oath to Hitler, promising to die at his command if need be. Adolf Hitler was now the complete warlord, the absolute dictator of Germany.
German: Pub. Hoffmann. No. T.4 1934. Value D.

77. Hitler in Weimar, July 1936

Hitler was fond of Weimar, in whose church he had held his first Reichstag (parliament) after his appointment as Chancellor in 1933. He even had a favourite rendezvous – the Elephant Hotel – and his hero, Frederick the Great, was buried in the town. It was in Weimar that the Republic, which had taken its name from the small Thuringian town, voted to give Hitler total authority to destroy the red (communist) peril, and thus voted itself out of existence. The occasion here is the 10th anniversary of the NSDAP Congress held at Weimar on 3–5 July 1926. At that time, Thuringia had been one of the few states where Hitler was allowed to speak in public.
German: Pub. Hoffmann. No. W4. 1936. Value B.

78. 'Einzug der Blutfahne' (Entry of the Blood Flag)

In the distant centre of this picture is the First World War memorial built between 1927 and 1930 to honour the 10,000 dead of Nuremberg. The memorial, repaired, still stands today, but the tribunes and other Nazi additions have been totally removed. This is the Luitpold Arena, less than 1 km from the Zeppelin Field, the other base for mass rallies. After the 1933 rally, when a wooden grandstand had been used, a labour force of over 600 men worked for twelve months to construct permanent accommodation to a design sketched by Adolf Hitler. The Führer is here walking immediately in front of the Blood Flag and in the ceremonies that followed, 75 new SS and 126 new SA Standards were inducted. The concluding march past took five hours. Hindenburg had died the month before, and so Hitler was, for the first time, conducting a rally as the absolute dictator of Germany.
German: Pub. F. Willmy, Nuremberg, 1934. Value D.

79

Der Führer spricht beim Appell auf der Zeppelinwiese vor 180 000 Politischen Leitern   SS·31

80

Nürnberg   Reichsparteitag S·A Lager Langwasser

81

DER EWIGE JUDE

GROSSE POLITISCHE SCHAU IM BIBLIOTHEKSBAU DES DEUTSCHEN MUSEUMS
ZU MÜNCHEN · AB 8. NOVEMBER 1937 · TÄGLICH GEÖFFNET VON 10-21 UHR

82

23.9.1933 Erfter Spatenftich
23.9.1936 1000 km Autobahn fertig

Poftkarte   Deutfche 6 +4 Reichspoft

83

79. Floodlit arena

This is the Zeppelin Field, floodlit by 130 Luftwaffe searchlights, their beams reaching 760 m (25,000 ft) into the night sky to form what was described as 'a cathedral of light'. The occasion was the evening of 7 September 1934 the 6th Nuremberg rally. In front of Hitler, who is standing on the podium by the flag, were 180,000 Nazi Party members and seated below the searchlights, 250,000 spectators. The whole rally was filmed by Leni Riefenstahl, and her resulting documentary 'Triumph of the Will', became a classic of film reportage. Despite the swamping adulation of the masses, Hitler was somewhat apprehensive about the rally. Less than three months earlier he had had the SA leader, Ernst Röhm, murdered in the killings of 'The Night of the Long Knives' and he was not wholly certain how the 100,000 SA rank and file involved in the rally, would behave. As a precaution, he had his own SS bodyguard, *Liebstandarte Adolf Hitler*, formed up around him, but the SA, under their new chief, Victor Lutze, demonstrated nothing but loyalty to their Führer.

German: Pub. Zerreis & Co., Nuremberg. No. 38/31, 1934. Value C.

80. Tented camp

This is the Langwasser camp area, just a few kilometres from the rally grounds. Each rally required an extraordinary amount of organisation, and the huge labour force – as well as the army of participants – was housed in this vast tented city. Each individual had an identifying number, a specific train or lorry to ride in, a specific seat in the train or lorry, a specific tent to live in, and a specific bed to sleep in. The postal arrangements were planned in equal detail. In 1935, the year that this card was posted, there was an official publicity slogan cancellation, two new stamps designed by Karl Diebitsch, a special greetings telegram, unknown numbers of official and unofficial postcards, three static post offices, twelve temporary ones, and one mobile. During the seven days of the rally, the German Post Office handled over 5½ million pieces of mail. This card, posted on 10 September 1935, carries the official 6Pf green stamp, and is cancelled with the official slogan. The written message is, 'Best wishes from the Reichsparteitag. Heil Hitler!'

German: Pub. Hoffmann. No. 5283, 1935. Value D.

81. The eternal Jew

Hitler professed in *Mein Kampf* that the way in which great leaders inspired their followers was to focus their attentions against one enemy. Hitler's choice was Judaism, and it was an extremely flexible one. Whenever the Nazis wished to attack a section of the community, or to make accusations against another country, they were able to claim that the Jews were always behind the scenes causing the trouble. The very internationality of the Jewish race made such Nazi propaganda plausible to those who wished to believe it. Eventually, the venomous hate of the Nazis for the Jews would lead to the mass deportations and the horrors of the concentration camps. Only marginally behind the Nazis'

oppression of the Jews, came their dislike of Communists, stemming from the days in 1919 when Red Brigades took control in many areas and not only threatened to overthrow the emerging Republic, but also to prevent Hitler's rise to power. Here the Jew is depicted as the grasping Shylock, out for his pound of flesh, and under his arm, complete with hammer and sickle, is tucked Germany. The card is an official government issue, advertising a political exhibition in the Munich Museum Library and carries a printed stamp on the reverse showing the head of Hindenburg. The cancellation includes the words *Der ewige Jude*.

German: Official card. Anti-Semitic Exhibition, Munich, November 1937. Value D.

Colour illustration on page 74.

82. Out!

Albert Einstein, possibly the world's greatest theoretical physicist, was born in Ulm in Germany in 1879, and began his schooling in Munich. By 1916 he was a professor at Berlin University and in 1922 received the Nobel prize for Physics. His interest in social affairs, and his ability to command an audience, made him a popular international figure. In 1932 he left Germany for a visit to California, and knowing that the Nazis were likely to come to power, he never returned. The painting is symbolic, using the figure of Einstein to represent the plight of all German Jews. The card was probably published in America in 1934. On the back in English is, presumably, a quote from Einstein: 'Neither hatred nor persecution can stay the progress of science and civilization'. The picture title is 'The Ignominy of the XXth Century'.

American: Artist M. Califano. Pub. anon. *Circa* 1934. Value D.

83 23 Sept. 1933: The first spadeful. 23 Sept. 1936: 1000 km of autobahn ready

Hitler's Germany was a one-party state and part of his solution to the massive problem of unemployment was to direct state funds into national projects. One such project was the building of wide, dual-carriageway roads between major population centres. The Italian Fascists had introduced their *autostrada* in the 1920s and now Hitler, shown on the postcard digging the first spadeful, began the autobahns. By 1938 over 3,000 km had been built, and an examination of the routes then covered by the autobahns, makes it clear that they had another object besides providing employment – they were able to supplement the role of the German railways in providing quick lines of internal communications for Hitler's armed forces. As always, Hitler's opening ceremony was timed to achieve maximum effect. September was the party month and 1936 the year of the Berlin Olympic Games. In the background are Julius Streicher, publisher of the anti-Semitic newspaper *Der Stürmer*, and Dr Todt, whose organisation supervised construction.

German: Pub. German Post Office, 1936. Value B.

FACKELSTAFFELLAUF OLYMPIA-BERLIN

84

XI. OLYMPISCHE SPIELE

BERLIN   1.-16. AUGUST 1936

85

Olympische Spiele 1936

Berlin 1.-16. August

Postkarte

Olympische Spiele
Berlin 1.-16. August
1936

6+4   4+6

Deutsches Reich

Familie

Oscar Miska

SCHL-ETTAU ueber Halle a.
Saale

Hallesche Salzwerke AG

86

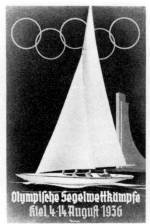

Olympische Segelwettkämpfe
Kiel, 4.-14. August 1936

Postkarte

6+4   4+6

Deutsches Reich

Herrn Diplm Kfmt

Otto Engwicht

Berlin W. 50

Passauer Str. 40 F. b. Kressis

87

Olympische Winterspiele
Garmisch-Partenkirchen
6.-16. Februar 1936

Postkarte

15+10   10+15

Deutsches Reich

88

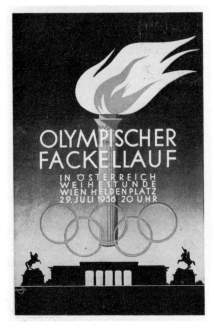

OLYMPISCHER
FACKELLAUF

IN ÖSTERREICH
WEIHESTUNDE
WIEN HELDENPLATZ
29. JULI 1936 20 UHR

89

[38]

84. Torch relay from Olympia to Berlin

The card shows an artist's impression of one of the German relay runners bringing the Olympic flame from Olympia to Berlin. The route is marked on the map behind. It was Hitler's intention that the 1936 Olympic Games should demonstrate to the world the superiority of German blood and the wonders of the Nazi State. This political exploitation of the Games produced a considerable reaction in America, where a movement was established to boycott the event – an oddly parallel situation to that of the Olympic Games held in Moscow in 1980. However, the movement did not succeed. Hitler's objective was not realised, despite world appreciation of the magnificence of the spectacle, the stadium and organisation, for in direct rebuff of the Nazi theory of the superiority of the fair-haired blue-eyed Teuton type, seven American negro athletes won gold medals. J.C. (Jesse) Owens won four golds, set two Olympic records and, with the 400 m relay team, broke the world record. The card has a printed title in German on the reverse: 'Propaganda card number 6 for the 1936 Olympic Games . . . proceeds to the Fund for German Sport'.
German: Pub. Reichssportverlag GmbH, Berlin. 1936. The card was cancelled on 16 August 1936 with the official Berlin Stadium mark. Value D.

85. 'XI Olympische Spiele, Berlin'. 1–16 August 1936

In order to attract the greatest number of foreign visitors to Berlin so that they could witness the hoped-for demonstration of Aryan athletic superiority, Hitler relaxed his anti-Jewish activities for the period of the Games. The Führer himself led the opening procession into the stadium, where an orchestra and chorus of over 3,000 voices led by Richard Strauss sang 'Deutschland Über Alles' and the 'Horst Wessel' song. This card was issued by the Austrian Olympic Committee to raise funds for its athletes and carries a printed message from the Committee's chairman.
Austrian: Pub. Austrian Olympic Committee, 1936. Value C.

86. 'Olympische Spiele' 1936

Although the Games did not substantiate Hitler's theories on the superiority of the Aryan race, Germany did win the most gold medals, pushing America into second place. The many foreign visitors who were attracted to Berlin, partly out of curiosity about the Nazi régime, went away impressed by the organisation and enthusiasm which they had seen.
German: Pub. German Post Office, 1936. Value B.

87. 'Olympische Segelwettkämpfe' (Olympic world sailing championship)

The sailing competitions took place at Kiel, and it had been there in 1918 that the mutiny of German sailors had sparked off the wave of socialist strikes that brought down the Kaiser. Germany won five of the seven rowing events, but only one sailing class. This card, in keeping with German philatelic tradition, was issued as an official collectors' item, and has been franked by a handstamp from a Dresden stamp exhibition, which ran concurrently with the Olympics. Card 59 carried a message about Mr Bartelmann and his rowing eight having an Olympic trial. If Bartelmann did make it to Kiel, his eight lost to the Americans, who won that class.
German: Pub. German Post Office. Value B.

88. 'Olympische Winterspiele' (Winter Olympic Games)

The winter Olympics were held in Garmisch Partenkirchen and Hitler was there to watch them. It was very much part of Hitler's familiar territory, lying in the shadow of the Zugspitze, Germany's highest mountain not far from Munich. The Nazis wrung effective worldwide propaganda from the whole Olympics. Special radio stations were established so that simultaneous foreign language commentaries could be broadcast, Leni Reifenstahl made a documentary film that obtained general release, and Hoffmann and his assistants took over 6,000 photographs.
German: Pub. German Post Office (1935). Value B.

89. 'Olympischer Fackellauf'

Card 84 shows the route of the runners bringing the Olympic flame to Berlin. This card, the Olympic flame in Austria, was produced as advance publicity for the passage of the torch through Vienna (Wien) and announced that it could be seen in the Heldenplatz at 8 p.m. on 29 July 1936. Since the opening ceremony was on 1 August that left two days to get to Berlin via Prague and Dresden.
Austrian: Pub. Austrian Committee for Olympic Victory. 1936. Value C.
Colour illustration on page 74.

Birth of the Axis 1936-1937

At the end of the First World War the seeds of the Second World War were sown. The Treaty of Versailles in 1919, confirmed the Armistice of 11 November 1918, and under pressure from the French, headed by Clemenceau, inflicted heavy financial reparations upon Germany. The British, among others, felt that the £6,000 million demanded was excessive, bearing in mind the territorial penalties also exacted. But the French were adamant, seeking revenge for their humiliation in 1871 and their million casualties on the Western Front. Thus Germans had a collective grudge against the treaty, a grudge that a strong leader could use to unite the nation. At the same time, following upon the creation of the League of Nations in 1920, there was abroad a great movement for peace. The League was charged by its charter to enforce peace by collective action, and although not all member nations formally signified their agreement of the League document, European politicians coloured all their actions by a wish to avoid war.

In three European countries the tensions following upon the war produced internal armed struggle, out of which grew three right-wing military dictatorships. These dictatorships, by using or by threatening force, were then able to capitalise upon the 'soft' actions of the other countries, who strove desperately to maintain the peace. The dictators were in Germany, Italy and Spain. On his way to power Adolf Hitler employed many of the techniques developed in Italy by Benito Mussolini, whom he admired. Once in power, he tested Germany's armed forces in international combat in the Spanish Civil War on the side of General Franco. Yet the three dictators did not join together. Franco remained aloof while Mussolini and Hitler formed the 'Axis'.

Mussolini had seized power in Italy on the back of a middle-class reaction to what seemed to be the growing strength of the working class. By coordinated strikes the workers had forced the employers to put up their wages at the expense of the salaried class whose net income was being eroded by inflation. Right-wing Italians were apprehensive about the spread of socialism from Russia and dissatisfied with the spoils of war handed out by the Versailles Treaty. In order to entice Italy into the First World War on their side, the British and French had promised Italy German territories which, in the end, she did not fully receive. In this sea of Italian discontent Mussolini's Fascist Blackshirts marched on Rome in October 1922 and King Victor Emmanuel handed the government over to Mussolini. Mussolini was now the leader (Il Duce) of Italy and virtually everyone supported him, either for nationalistic reasons, anti-Bolshevist reasons or because of the skilful and emotive propaganda that gave the mass of the people a warm feeling of belonging to something 'glorious'.

At first Mussolini seemed prepared to collaborate with the different interests within the nation – the Church, the King, the political parties, the Freemasons, the press and parliament. But by 1925 he had assumed total power and that same year established a secret police whose function was to ensure the continuance of his own rule – a parallel with Hitler's later introduction of the SS. Italy became a one-party State eight years before Adolf Hitler was appointed Chancellor of Germany.

By 1932 the effects of the Depression were being as badly felt in Italy as elsewhere. The government reduced the working week and spent great sums of money on public works. The railways were electrified and great new roads named *autostrada* were begun (an idea later copied by Hitler with his autobahns) but it was only by colonial adventurism that Il Duce was able to reduce unemployment. He went to war in Ethiopia (Abyssinia).

'Better to live one day as a lion than a thousand years as a lamb', said Mussolini in 1935. It is almost a standard rule of a totalitarian state that if things are bad at home the best way to divert the people's attention away from their troubles is to fight an overseas war. Mussolini had been building up the armed forces, partly to bolster his dream of re-creating Roman glories, and partly to stimulate industry, and when he invaded Ethiopia in October 1935 it was an uneven contest: a modern industrial country with aeroplanes and sophisticated weapons against a backward and almost native country. By the middle of 1936 the war was over and even the temporary sanctions imposed by the League of Nations against Italy were lifted. Ethiopia was amalgamated with Italian Somaliland and Eritrea to form Italian East Africa. A dictator had demonstrated that the peace-mongers of the League of Nations would give way to a show of strength, and another dictator, named Adolf Hitler, was watching and learning. It was time that the Führer of resurgent Germany made his mark on the international stage. He had promised his people that he would overthrow the Versailles Treaty. Now he could take his first step.

On 7 March 1936 Hitler's forces marched into the Rhineland. Confident, in view of the League of Nations failure to stop Mussolini in Ethiopia, that he would be unopposed, Hitler 'took back' the territory between the Rhine and the French border that had been forfeited under the Versailles Treaty. The German people were overjoyed. Their Führer was not only solving economic problems at home but was also now beginning the process of restoring to Germany the lost lands. The French, frightened by the move, sought Britain's help to resist. Britain, concerned with peace, and inclined to think that the territory *was* German anyway, refused. Hitler had won, but he knew that his forces were not good enough to take on Britain and France together. If they had opposed him he would have lost. His forces must be trained in combat and an opportunity to do just that was only a few months away – in Spain.

In 1930, Primo de Rivera, who had been virtual dictator of Spain for seven years, resigned. In reaction to the sudden loss of central authoritarian control, republican and communist movements struggled for power. In February 1936 a communist-supported Popular Front won national elections, and right-wing military garrisons around Spain rose in revolt, led by General Francisco Franco, previously exiled by the Socialist government. The right-wing rebels conducted open warfare against the forces loyal to the Socialist Popular Front. Russia supplied and reinforced the loyalists and Franco sought aid from Italy and Germany. The Spanish General's plea for help reached Hitler on 22 July. His urgent need was for aeroplanes. Hitler consulted Goering, the head of the Luftwaffe, and he enthusiastically gave his support in order to, 'test my young air force'. Transport aeroplanes and experimental fighter and anti-aircraft units were soon on their way. It was a rehearsal for a war that was to come, it was the making of the *blitzkrieg* ('lightning war') that was to ravage the Continent three years later, when the peaceful statesmen of Europe said 'That's Enough'! But they gave in to Hitler several times more before they found the courage to stand up to him.

"LE TIGRE"

90

PNF DOPOLAVORO OND
FORZE ARMATE

91

IV ADUNATA NAZIONALE
ARMA DEL GENIO
FIRENZE 23-25 MAGGIO 1936 XIV
ASSOCIAZIONE NAZIONALE
DELL'ARMA

92

93

94

90. 'Le Tigre'

This fiery, seemingly indestructible statesman well deserved his nickname, 'Tiger'. In 1917, at the age of 78, Georges Clemenceau became France's Premier for the second time, and thus played a leading role in imposing the harsh terms of the Treaty of Versailles.

Lloyd George, his British counterpart during the First World War, described Clemenceau's attitude to Germany thus, 'His hatred of Germany had a concentrated ferocity which I had never seen before, not even among the most violent of our British Germanophobes. Their hostility to Germany always seemed to be calculated and histrionic – his was of the blood.' These violent feelings stemmed back to the Franco-Prussian War of 1870, when Clemenceau was Mayor of Montmartre, Paris. In 1871 he was elected a member of the National Assembly, and one of his enduring memories was of Minister of Defence, Jules Favre, reporting to the Assembly the harshness of the terms demanded by Bismarck from vanquished France. Favre wept as he described the German demands, and the memory, according to Lloyd George, 'had rankled in the heart of this fierce old patriot for 50 years'.

Clemenceau's moment of sweet revenge came on 28 June 1919 when he opened the proceedings at which the German delegation, Dr Müller and Dr Bell, signed the Treaty of Versailles. 'Gentlemen', he barked, 'the session is open. We are here to sign a Treaty of Peace.' Cannons boomed outside as the Germans signed. 'The session is closed' – Clemenceau brought the proceedings to an abrupt end. Painlevé, one of the French delegates, congratulated him. Onlookers reported tears in the bleary old eyes as he replied, 'Yes, it's a beautiful day'. But the oppressive terms of that treaty may well be described as the direct cause of the Second World War.

This delightful caricature of Clemenceau, 'Le Tigre', is by Bert Thomas, a First World War artist who went on to draw anti-Hitler and 'ITMA' cartoons during the Second World War

British: Pub. Odhams Ltd. Artist Bert Thomas. *Circa* 1919. Value C.

91. 'Il Duce and Victor Emmanuel III: After toil, strength in arms'

In his delusions of grandeur, Mussolini saw himself re-creating the glory that was the Roman Empire. 'The twentieth century will be the century of Fascism, of Italian power, during which Italy will return for the third time to be the directing force in human civilization,' he proclaimed in 1932.

The main target for his imperialist expansion plans was East Africa. In 1935, Italy had 250,000 men under arms in East Africa and Eritrea was made the base for the conquest of Ethiopia. Despite strenuous efforts by Britain to negotiate a settlement, the Italians invaded on 3 October 1935.

When Addis Ababa fell on 5 May 1936, Mussolini declared Victor Emmanuel III (without consulting him) Emperor, to mark the establishment of Italian suzerainty over Ethiopia. This postcard celebrates the event. Pursuing a policy of what appeared to the world to be, 'if you can't beat 'em, join 'em', Victor Emmanuel acquiesced with Mussolini and his Fascist policies, signing decrees that virtually eliminated his own power and the freedom of the Press.

The letters 'PNF' mean National Fascist Party.
Italian: Pub. 'IGAP', Roma. Artist Lalia, 1936. Value C.

92. 'IV Adunata Nazionale'

Mussolini had developed his technique of mass persuasion through pomp and ceremony well before Hitler, and the Führer learned much from Il Duce. This card celebrates the 4th National Rally of the Army Engineers, held on 23–25 May 1936 in Florence, but the event of the year was the Olympic Games in Berlin.
Italian: Pub. ANAG. The National Army League, Artist Virgilio Retrosi. Posted 10 December 1936. Value C.

93. 'Implacabile'

This splendidly dramatic coloured card commemorates the battle honours of the 301st and 311th Mountain Sections of the Italian First Division. The honours were won during the Ethiopian (Abyssinian) campaign of 1935/36, when modern Italian forces using machine guns, aeroplanes and poison gas subdued a native population. The ease of their success gave Mussolini and his forces an inflated idea of their military capabilities and this is reflected in the exuberance of the postcard picture.
Italian: Pub. V. E. Boeri. *Circa* 1939. Value C.
Colour illustration on page 74.

94. Symbolic eagle

This is an official Fascist propaganda card, according to the legend on the back. The *Encyclopaedia Britannica* defines Fascism as 'a political attitude which puts the nation-state or the race, its power and growth, in the centre of life and history'. Fascism has become synonymous with the name and career of Benito Mussolini in Italy, but Hitler and his National Socialism, and Franco and his Falangism, were also exponents of this fanatical political ideology. The main tenets of Mussolini's Fascism are set out on the eagle – patriotism, faith, obedience and belief in the infallibility of Il Duce predominate. This latter concept proved an increasingly weak foundation upon which to build Italian fortunes as Mussolini's policies began to depend less upon his intuition and more upon his whimsy.
Italian: Pub. Acta Milan. Artist Boccasile (the Fascist movement's official artist). *Circa* 1935. Value B.

95

96

70° REGGIMENTO FANTERIA
=ANCONA= AFRICA ORIENTALE

97

QUALE ORGOGLIO DEVE VIBRARE NEI CUORI DELLE CAMICIE NERE
D'ITALIA, CHE SONO STATE LE PRIME A COMBATTERE IL BOLSCEVISMO,
CHE VI HANNO OPPOSTO LA BARRIERA DEI LORO PETTI, CHE HANNO
GUARITO L'ITALIA E DALL'ITALIA SEGNATO LA VIA DELLA SALVEZZA
ALL'EUROPA.
Da "IL POPOLO D'ITALIA" - 13-6-1937-XV

98

VIII°·btg.arabo-somalo

T. Col. Rotti

99

1ª ADUNATA A ROMA
DELLE TRUPPE
COLONIALI PER IL
1º ANNIVERSARIO
DELLA FONDAZIONE
DELL'IMPERO
9 MAGGIO 1936 - XIV
9 MAGGIO 1937 - XV

100

95. 'Sull'Amba Ed Oltre'

The title translates as 'On the Amba and beyond'. The card acknowledges the prowess of the XII Colonial Artillery Group, and its pack artillery, during the assault in 1936 on the Amba, an Ethiopian mountain. It seems quite likely that the Italian Colonial soldiers in the XII Group, such as those pictured here, originated from either Eritrea (an Italian province since 1890) or Somaliland (Italian since 1889). These countries isolated Ethiopia from the sea and their citizens were familiar with the terrain and climate inland, and were therefore better able to cope with difficult features than imported European Italians.
Italian: Pub. V. E. Boeri Rome. Artist D'Ercoli. *Circa* 1938. Value C.

96. 'XXXV Come Falco Sulla Preda'

Another of artist D'Ercoli's coloured flights of fancy, showing the 35th Colonial Battalion (motto: 'like a hawk after its prey') in action in Ethiopia. The three-bladed sword carries the names of battle honours including Adua (Aduwa), the Ethiopian town captured by the Italians on 6 October 1935, just three days after their invasion began, and thirty-nine years after a humiliating defeat there by native warriors.
Italian: Pub. V. E. Boeri, Rome. Artist D'Ercoli. *Circa* 1939. Value C.

97. '70th Reggimento Fanteria – Ancona'

Further dramatic representation of Italy's over-estimated military success in East Africa, this card commemorates the victory of the joint Italian and Colonial 70th Infantry Regiment at the battle of Ancona on 6 October 1935. Before the turn of the century, Italian expansionist martial expeditions in East Africa had met with little success, mainly due to the incompetence of Baratieri, the commanding general involved. At the battle of Adua (Ethiopia) in March 1896, Baratieri and 6,000 Italians were completely routed by native troops. The memorial obelisk in the picture says 'The defeat at Adua on 1 March 1896 has been revenged by the victory of 6.X.1935'.
Italian: Pub. V. E. Boeri, Rome. Artist La Monaca. *Circa* 1936. Value C.

98. Blackshirts

Following the end of the First World War, aggressive socialism – in its extreme form of bolshevism – was blown across Europe by the explosive force of the Russian Revolution. In Spain, Germany and Italy, armed internal struggles between the Bolsheviks and the extreme right, to gain power, led eventually to the establishment of right-wing dictatorships in those countries. Minor territorial differences between Mussolini and Hitler, such as that over South Tyrol, were sublimated to their common fear and hatred of bolshevism. Here the Blackshirts ('the first to fight bolshevism'), Mussolini's Fascists (the black motif was later adopted for Mosley's followers in Britain and the SS in Germany), are in armed confrontation with the unseen bolshevik enemy.
Italian: Pub. Acta. Milan. Artist Matelli. *Circa* 1937. Value C.

99. 'VIII Btg. Arabo-Somalo'

Most Italian regiments seem to have their own postcards. Sometimes large companies in the areas of Italy from which a regiment drew its main strength, would subsidise a card which soldiers could have free, or for very little money. The actions of 1935/1936 were used by Mussolini to bolster his reputation at home by emphasising Italy's place in world affairs as a colonial power. This card is a regimental one for the VIII Somali Battalion, the 'Leopard' battalion. Somalia lies between Ethiopia and the Indian Ocean and was a springboard for the October 1935 invasion.
Italian: Pub. V. E. Boeri, Rome. Artist Grotti. *Circa* 1936. Value B.

100. '1st Adunata'

The card commemorates the first anniversary of the conquest of Ethiopia in 1936 and the adoption by Victor Emmanuel III, on 9 May 1936, of the title 'Emperor of Ethiopia'. The inscription has the period printed as '9 Maggio 1936-XIV' to '9 Maggio 1937-XV'. The additional numbers XIV and XV relate to the year of Mussolini's accession. He came to power in 1922, and so 1936 is year XIV and 1937 is year XV. Interestingly, the troops taking part in the Rome rally included some of the colonial forces who fought in the Ethiopia campaign.
Italian: Pub. V. E. Boeri, Rome. *Circa* 1937. Value C.

101

102

103

10

105

10

Der FÜHRER und der DUCE
„Die Garanten des Friedens"

107

103, 104, 105, 106. Four cards

The pictures are doubtless part of a large series of cards depicting life in the Italian African colonies. The regular routine of the Italian soldier in Africa would not have been any different to his equivalent in any other European army. The cards show a church parade, a march past with band and colours, and scenes of locals. This particular group of cards was issued from the soldiers' rest home in Asmara for the 128th Legion of the 5th Division, probably in the late 1920s. Asmara was the capital of the Italian territory of Eritrea, and, being situated on a high plateau some 64 km (40 miles) inland from the Red Sea, was a natural place for military and government headquarters. It formed the main support area for the invasion of Ethiopia in 1935 and then became the principal city of Italy's new African empire.

Italian: Pub. Fedetto, Turin. *Circa* 1929. Each card value A.

107. 'Der Führer und der Duce'

Hitler and Mussolini first met in 1934. After the German leader's accession to the Chancellorship in February 1933, France and Russia noted with alarm his obvious intention to re-arm. They therefore opened negotiations for a pact of mutual defence, and by April 1934 seemed near to agreement. Hitler, fearing that Germany would be sandwiched alone between her old enemies, looked for a friend. Although Mussolini had not lent the money the Nazis had asked for in 1924, and the two countries were in dispute about South Tyrol, the Italian dictator was undoubtedly Hitler's best bet. Hitler had, after all, admired and copied many of Il Duce's techniques of crowd manipulation and ceremonial. They were both right-wing dictators. Thus a meeting was arranged, and on 14 June 1934 Hitler landed at Venice's Lido airfield, wearing civilian clothes. He was greeted and upstaged by a flamboyant Mussolini in a black and gold uniform. The visit was not a success and Hitler did not get any promise of Italian support. But the Spanish Civil War of 1936 was clear evidence of the dangerous strength of bolshevism, and both dictators felt a need for each other's support. Thus a secret treaty of collaboration between Italy and Germany was signed in Berlin in October 1936, and was described by Mussolini as an, 'axis around which can revolve all those European states with a will to collaboration and peace'. On 25 September 1937 Mussolini arrived at Munich railway station to visit Hitler, and this card records the moment of their meeting. At the end of several days of close contact, the two dictators parted with equal regard each for the other, and a professed policy of co-operation that made Mussolini's 'Axis' a reality.

German: Pub. Hoffmann. No. M.10. 1937. Value C.

101. 'Buon Natale'

Buon Natale means Happy Christmas, and this card was sent to Italy by a soldier of the Italian Expeditionary force based in Tobruk, in December 1937. Italy by this time had large areas of north and north-east Africa under her control – albeit mostly desert – and Mussolini was in the fullest flush of his swaggering role as successful dictator and world statesman. Whether African natives would have genuinely welcomed Italian aeroplanes in the way that the drawing suggests, is very much open to doubt!

Italian: Pub. Armetti, Milan. *Circa* 1937. Value B.

102. 'Centenario Fondazione Dei Bersaglieri, 1836–1936'

The *Bersaglieri*, or marksmen, were an élite branch of Italian light infantry, first formed in Sardinia in 1836. They performed well in various campaigns before the First World War, by which time they were well known for their fast marching and elegant plumed hats. Mussolini served in the Bersaglieri as a private during the First World War and they always played a prominent role on ceremonial occasions. The card commemorates the 100th anniversary of their formation.

Italian: Pub. Diena. 1936. Value B.

108

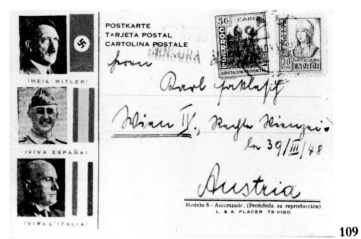

109

111

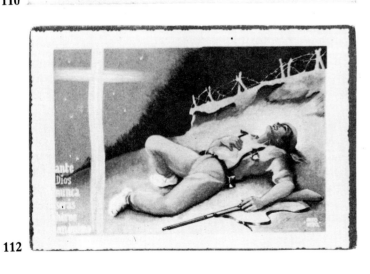

110

112

113

108. Hitler and Franco

In 1936 the left-wing Republican Popular Front Party came to power in Spain and introduced reforms which prompted a 17 July right-wing military revolt led by Nationalist General Francisco Franco. Just two months earlier Mussolini had successfully concluded his war in Ethiopia. Hitler, impressed by Italian flouting of the League of Nations' disapproval of its Ethiopian campaign, and knowing that Mussolini supported Franco, decided that he too would back the General. In September Luftwaffe planes arrived in Spain, followed by Italian infantry and light tanks. If Franco gained control of Spain, Hitler could see the possibility of having bases on the southern borders of France. These would be powerful deterrents to French opposition to German plans of expansion. Hitler did not actually meet Franco until October 1940 and was then unable to persuade the Spaniard to co-operate. This card is not contemporary to the 1940 meeting it depicts, but was part of a 1947 postal campaign directed at United Nations Secretary General Trygve Lie requesting action against Nazi elements in Spain.
Spanish: 1947. Value B.

109. Hitler, Franco and Mussolini

The war in Spain between the left-wing Republicans and Franco's right-wing Nationalists dragged on for three years. The governments of Franco's two friendly dictators recognised his régime in November 1936 and supported him through to final victory. For the Germans it was an opportunity to practise their armed forces in modern warfare and to develop the concept of ground and air co-operation between tanks and aeroplanes that produced the lightning war – *blitzkrieg*.
Spanish: Pub. L & A Placer. 1937. Value C.
Colour illustration on page 74.

110. Franco. 'Arriba España!'

The Spanish Civil War lasted almost three years. During that time each side, the Nationalist rebels under Franco and the Loyalist supporters of the Socialist government, administered the areas under their control. This is an 'official' rebel card commemorating the first anniversary of the revolution, and was sold as a fund raiser for the cause. The war had begun following a clash between the Spanish Foreign Legion and a communist mob in Spanish Morocco. This card carries stamps titled '17 July 1936 National Uprising' and is cancelled 17 July 1937 in Tetuan, Morocco. The stamps were produced by Waterlow and Sons, London and designed by M. Bertuchi. *Arriba Espana!* means 'Spain above all!'
Spanish: Pub. Spanish Rebel Forces. 1937. Value C.

111. Colonel Moscardo

The revolution in Spain was a military one against the elected, communist-influenced, popular front government. Five cities in Morocco and twelve in mainland Spain rose against the government. The cadets at the Toledo Military Academy near Madrid followed their commandant, Colonel José Moscardo, who declared for the rebels. The Academy was besieged by Loyalist militiamen for two months before being relieved on 28 September 1936. This card was posted in Seville on 1 November 1937.
Spanish: Pub. Spanish Rebel Forces. 1937. Value B.

112. A dead soldier

The Spanish Civil War was a visible symptom of the ideological struggle between the political doctrines of extreme left and extreme right that had been set into violent motion by the Russian Revolution. As the Socialist government struggled against the military rebels, sympathisers flocked to Spain from around the world to help to put down the rightist revolt. They formed themselves into International Brigades and found support from Soviet Russia. Mussolini, flushed by easy success in Ethiopia, and Hitler, looking for a foothold on the Mediterranean, supported Franco. Communism confronted Fascism. Eventually Fascism won and in the process Hitler trained his army for war. In 1938 all the International Brigades were sent home and this card published in Barcelona, one of the last socialist strongholds, may be an acknowledgement of the government's debt to its unknown foreign friends who gave their lives for the cause. The caption says 'Before God none are unknown'.
Spanish: Pub. Popular Front. *Circa* 1938. Value D.

113. 'Viva Espana!'

Prominent among the Spanish and revolutionary flags are those of Germany and Italy. Both countries gave massive support to Franco – probably much more than they had originally intended to give when the revolt began. Italy provided mostly fully equipped infantry divisions totalling over 50,000 men, although her contribution to the air war is said to have exceeded 1,000 aircraft. Mussolini gained little if anything from his participation in the war. Vast quantities of material were expended, and the Blackshirts suffered some humiliating defeats.
Spanish: Pub. Arribas. *Circa* 1938. Value C.
Colour illustration on page 74.

114

115

116

LA AMENAZA AÉREA DE ALEMANIA

radio de acción de los aviones de bombardeo.

1 avión = 250 aviones de guerra.

117

118

119

114. Condor Legion flags

Adolf Hitler did not commit his armed forces to a major, face-to-face, conflict in Spain in the way that Mussolini did. German efforts were mainly in air support, though some artillery and armour were provided, and 26,113 German military personnel were decorated by Hitler for 'meritorious conduct' during the war. The Führer did act quickly, however, and twenty-six aircraft with their crews were sent to Spain in August 1936. This small force, known as the Legion Condor (LC), expanded into an air arm of considerable size, commanded by General Wolfram von Richthofen, a cousin of the First World War 'Red Baron'. Close air support techniques in aid of ground forces were developed, which later were to form the basis of the lightning war of 1939 and 1940. This card was issued to commemorate the return to Germany of the Legion Condor in June 1939, following the end of the war in Spain. On the reverse it carries a Berlin handstamp for 6 June 1939 with the words (in German), 'Homecoming of the Legion Condor'.
German: Pub. T. Konig, Berlin. 1939. Value D.

115. Tanks and aeroplanes

This artist's impression of tanks and aeroplanes co-operating in an attack is a pictorial summary of the major benefit that Germany gained from the Spanish Civil War. Close co-operation techniques between mobile ground forces and aeroplanes using radio telephones were devised, leading ultimately to the blitzkrieg of 1939 and 1940. The aeroplanes are probably meant to represent the Heinkel (He) 51, the first Luftwaffe fighter to be built in large numbers. More than thirty He51 aircraft served with the Legion Condor and in total over 100 were used in Spain in one form or another. The tank resembles the *Panzerkampfwagen* 11 (Pz11) whose gun could fire both armour piercing and high explosive ammunition. The Pz11 came into use early in 1936, though it did not serve in Spain.
German: Pub. Leutert and Schneiderwind, Dresden. *Circa* 1937. Value C.
Colour illustration on page 74.

116. Dive bombers

Perhaps the most dreaded product of the war in Spain was the dive bomber. Early bomb attacks by He51s from as low as 150 m (500 ft) were developed into accurate diving runs by the Junkers (JU) 87A and the Henschel 123. The aircraft in this picture are JU87A 'Stuka' dive-bombers, which were used in Spain from 1937. Apart from the effectiveness of its weapons, the aircraft's angular appearance and high engine scream when in a dive added to the terror it inspired. The name 'Stuka' comes from *Sturzkampfflugzeug*, meaning 'dive-bomber'.
German: Pub. Grieshaber and Sauberlich, Stuttgart. *Circa* 1939. Value C.

117. 'La Amenaza Aérea de Alemania'

This is a German propaganda card distributed via the German Embassy in Portugal. The theme is that Germany is under threat and must re-arm in order to defend herself.

Here the menace is in the air, as the title says. The whole of Germany can be reached by the warplanes of her neighbours and since one small symbolic aeroplane represents 250 aircraft, the total threat claimed is:

Poland	1,000	aircraft
Czechoslovakia	750	aircraft
France	4,500	aircraft
Belgium	250	aircraft

The map also shows very clearly how Polish territory stretched up to Danzig on the North Sea, thus forming a 'corridor' between the very top of Germany (East Prussia) and Germany herself.
German: Pub. German Propaganda Ministry. *Circa* 1937. Value C.

118. 'LS Graf Zeppelin'

LS (*Luft Schiffe* – air ship) 'Graf Zepplin' was a formidable symbol of German engineering skill. Within a few weeks of her first flight in 1928, she began a regular commercial service that was to last for more than eight years. Her total flying hours exceeded 17,000, she travelled over 1.6 million km (1 million miles) and carried some 13,000 fare-paying passengers. Although designed and operated purely as a commercial craft, she provided valuable training in airframe construction for those who would later build the Luftwaffe. The figure on the card is Heinrich von Stephan, the centenary of whose birth in 1931 is the reason for the card's publication. Stephan is credited with being the inventor of the postcard, and first suggested the idea in 1865.
German: Pub. German Post Office. Card flown on the 'LS Graf Zeppelin' August 1931. Value D.

119. Nazi airship

The Treaty of Versailles severely limited Germany's freedom to develop and maintain military aircraft. Despite this, and well before Hitler came to power, determined individuals like General Hans von Seeckt, Chief of Army Command, found ways of keeping military aviation alive. Apart from the purely military aspects of aerial technology, prowess in the air became a symbol of a country's standing, an indicator of its worth, and symbolism was all-important to the NSDAP. In 1926, by the Treaty of Paris, the German aircraft industry was given freedom of development. Two years later, on 18 September 1928, the 'Graf Zeppelin' took off on her first flight. The whole nation saw her as a symbol of a resurgent Germany, and throughout 1927 and 1928 public money had flowed in to help the development. At the end of 1934, following Hitler's rise to the Chancellorship, another and bigger Zeppelin was laid down. The greatest volume dirigible yet built, she offered passengers more *Lebensraum* (living room), an expression that Hitler was to use to describe the annexations of 1936 to 1939. That airship was the 'Hindenburg', seen here at Frankfurt. The swastikas on the tail were part of Nazi propaganda for the March 1936 referendum. The airship followed the Führer from town to town. Hitler obtained 99 per cent of the votes.
German: Pub. Franz Harz. 1936. Value C.

120

Deutsche Luftfahrt

Nach Motiven deutscher Briefmarken

121

MUCHAS FELICIDADES

VIA CONDOR – LUFTHANSA

122

123

120. 'Deutsche Luftfahrt'

By 1936, when this card was issued, German aviation (the title here) was strong and vigorous. Commercial development of air travel, aside from Germany's underlying military intentions, was aimed at passengers, post and, to a lesser degree, freight. The airship is LS. 129, the Hindenburg, carrying the Olympic rings. She flew over the stadium as part of the Nazi 'Master Race' propaganda. The figure to the right is Graf von Zeppelin. On the left is Professor Hugo Junkers, founder of the Junkers aircraft works. Below him is a three-engined Junkers JU52, which was produced as a transport aircraft for Lufthansa and as a bomber for the Luftwaffe, flying with the Hindenburg squadron during the Spanish Civil War.
German: Pub. German Post Office. 1936. Value D.

121. 'Via Condor' – Lufthansa

At the end of the First World War, over 15,000 of Germany's 20,000 military aircraft had to be surrendered to the Allies. Restrictions were placed upon the development of civil aircraft for a short time, but these were lifted in 1926. In the early 1920s a small group of officers, led by General Hans von Seeckt, had established a covert plan to direct the resurrection of a German air force (*luftwaffe*), and their method was to use the permitted development of commercial aeroplanes to hide their real intentions. The State airline, Lufthansa, had been formed in 1926, on the relaxation of restrictions. Its Chairman was Erhard Milch, and under his direction it became the best equipped and trained airline in Europe, interest and innovation being stimulated by flying displays and local flying clubs. International routes, such as the Condor route (*Via Condor*), were established around the world. The Condor route was to Spanish-speaking South America and named after the world's largest flying bird, which is found there. When the Luftwaffe sent its planes to Spain, they too took the name, and became the *Legion Condor*.
German: Pub. Lufthansa. *Circa* 1936. Value D.
Colour illustration on page 75.

122. Hitler and Co.

At the head of this group of Nazi officers, walking across the airfield, are Hitler and Goering. The latter, a First World War pilot who had won the coveted *Pour le Mérite*, was an early, steadfast, supporter of Hitler. In April 1933 he was appointed Air Minister, with Lufthansa head, Milch, as his deputy. Although most overt and covert development of Lufthansa was pioneered by Milch, when Hitler officially announced the existence of the Luftwaffe in March 1935, Goering was appointed to command it, with the rank of Colonel-General. Immediately Goering set out to establish a high *esprit de corps* among his airmen, often slighting the army in the process, but in the years of the Spanish Civil War his Legion Condor developed the air-to-ground tactics, in conjunction with the army, that were to prove so deadly in 1939/40.

German: Pub. Hoffmann. No. 864 (*Circa* 1936).

123. Goebbels and Co.

Hitler and his immediate entourage made great use of the aeroplane for travelling around the country. This grassy airfield is in Königsberg, the capital of East Prussia, and Goebbels is carrying a bunch of flowers. The occasion may, therefore, have been a visit by the Propaganda Minister to speak to the local party faithful, whose leaders turned out to welcome him with flowers. In the background is one of Hermann Goering's own aircraft. The involvement of high party officials with the aeroplane added to the aggressive impetus of development that led to the building of new runways and airport facilities.

German: Pub. Wehrmacht. Field Post Card. *Circa* 1937. Value B.

House of German Art
(Haus der Deutschen Kunst) 1937

Hitler was an artist *manqué*. The image of a crude house painter and decorator called Schicklgruber was a particularly effective Allied propaganda story during the Second World War. Certainly, Hitler's paternal grandmother, Maria Ann Schicklgruber, gave birth to an illegitimate baby, Alois. There are rumours that the baby's un-named father was the wealthy Jew for whom Maria Ann worked. (It is ironic that the criminally anti-Semitic Adolf Hitler may well have had Jewish blood in his veins.) When Alois was 5, his mother married a man called Johann Georg Heidler, but, when she died five years later, Heidler left his stepson. Alois was then brought up by Heidler's brother, Johann Nepomuk Heidler. In a complicated attempt to legitimise Alois, his birth registration was changed. 'Illegitimate' was altered to 'legitimate', and 'Georg Hitler' was acknowledged as the father. The slight alteration of 'Heidler' to 'Hitler' was accepted, and so the future Adolf's surname was arrived at.

The young Adolf's pedigree was equally complicated. His father married, for a second time, a girl who had been his mistress while he was still married to his first wife. Because of the strange legitimisation process, the girl, Klara Pölzl, who was Johan Nepomuk Heidler's granddaughter, was his technical niece. Because she was already pregnant, Alois got a special dispensation to marry her. Adolf was their fourth child and the first to survive. So much for his parentage and his name.

As far as his artistic pretensions were concerned, he developed a talent and liking for sketching. At the age of sixteen, he left school, and for the next few years he drifted, jobless, in Linz, painting, sketching and visiting the opera. Gradually his drawings changed emphasis – he discovered that he wanted to be an architect. He persuaded his mother, now sick with the cancer that would kill her, to allow him to spend his father's legacy on a year's tuition at the Vienna Academy. Adolf failed his first art exam miserably, which only convinced him that architecture was his métier. He returned home to Linz, despairing of being able to enter the School of Architecture, to nurse his dying mother. She died on 21 December 1907, leaving Hitler grief-stricken. Two months later he returned to Vienna, but he was rejected by the Academy. It was a lean time for the failed young artist. Nevertheless, he always found enough money to visit the opera and his life-long love of Wagner was kindled during this period. A second application to the Academy only produced another rejection. By the end of the year he had spent the last of his patrimony and was forced to rely on charity. He sold a few postcards – city scenes, copies of photographs – and had some success with larger water colours. The proceeds kept the wolf from the door, and in the autumn of 1910 he applied yet again to enter the Academy of Fine Arts. Yet again he was rejected. Hitler then entered a steadier period, producing pencil sketches, water colours and paintings – most of which he sold to dealers.

In 1913 he left Vienna for Munich, and immediately started work again on his paintings. He found them more difficult to sell than in Vienna, and the Munich Art Academy as disinterested in him as was

Vienna's. He enjoyed, however, the artistic bohemian society of the Schwabing district, and managed to sell some pictures in Munich's popular *Bierkellers*.

His abortive professional artistic career was finally nipped in its dying bud by the outbreak of the First World War and Hitler immediately joined up in the Bavarian Infantry. The drawing, however, continued. Like Bruce Bairnsfather (the British artist whose droll pictures, known as 'Fragments from France', relieved the misery of his fellow soldiers in the hellish trenches of 'Plugstreet' Wood in Flanders), Hitler also drew cartoons on postcards to amuse his comrades – not 5 km away in 'Whitesheet'.

The Iron Cross 1st class winner also painted watercolours (some of which have survived and are in the Library of Congress, Washington, DC) of the ruined Flemish landscapes and battle scenes he had witnessed. Hilter's post-war obsession with politics and his scramble to power left little time for art. Once established as Reich Chancellor, however, and with virtually limitless funds at his disposal, Hitler was able to indulge in the vicarious artistic pleasure of patronising, furthering and collecting his own, hugely subjective version of 'art'.

His obsession with anti-Semitism and his narrow, somewhat puritanical moral outlook obscured his judgement and artistic taste. All art which did not conform to his classical, romantic, stereotyped concept was classified as 'decadent' or 'degenerate'. Into this category came not only all works by Jewish, negro, and communist artists but also modern, abstract, expressionist or 'experimental' designs. The famous artistic workshop formed by Walter Gropius in 1919 and known as the Bauhaus, was disbanded by Hitler in 1933. The craftsmen, artists, architects and designers who worked with Gropius were also on Hitler's proscribed list. They included Feininger, Klee, Kandinsky and Mondrian. The whole modern field of expressionism, including the Berlin and Vienna Secessionists, was frowned upon by Hitler. So were brilliant international artists like Chagall, Matisse, Picasso, Van Gogh, Braque, Kokoshka, Kirchner and Schiele. Emil Nolde, who like Hitler had kept body and soul together in his youth by selling postcard designs (of mountains personified by grotesque faces), was among the despised, even though he was a Nazi sympathiser. Albert Speer, given the task of decorating Goebbels' new house in 1933, hung several Nolde watercolours. The Goebbels were delighted – until Hitler saw them, expressed his displeasure, and Goebbels told Speer: 'The pictures have to go at once; they're simply impossible.' Goebbels, Speer, and any other of Hitler's intimates with any pretensions to artistic or intellectual tastes, had to stifle their own preferences and bow to the Führer's blanket view of what constituted 'degeneracy'.

A team of approved artists and experts, including Professor Adolf Ziegler (President of the National Art Council) and Wolf Willrich (q.v.) (who went on to portray many Nazi personalities) toured art galleries and museums throughout the country, searching out 'degenerate' art. Their haul was estimated at over 16,000 works of art – sculptures as well as paintings and sketches, by the types of artist described above; 1,000 of Nolde's pictures alone were confiscated. In 1937 controversial items were shown in an 'Exhibition of Degenerate Work' in Munich by Goebbels, who had been created President of the Reich Chamber of Culture, with responsibility for the arts and entertainment media. The exhibition proved immensely popular, and crowds flocked to get a last look at some superb works of art (rather than to jeer at 'Yiddish obscenity', as was the object of the exhibition) as it toured the country. Even Hoffmann, Hitler's official photographer and personal friend, broke his usual policy of not upsetting Hitler by protesting at some of the inclusions in this exhibition. He even went so far as to venture the comment that Goebbels, 'would be much better advised to concentrate his attack on artistic trash, and particularly some of the trash which we ourselves are producing. Of the pictures submitted for acceptance in *Das Haus der Deutschen Kunst*, at least one-third come into this category. Many artists seem to think that as long as the national flag, the swastika, heaps of party uniforms and standards, masses of uniformed SA and SS and Hitler Youth on the march are included in a picture, that in itself gives it a right to demand acceptance!' Hoffmann's remarks were more than justified, and even Hoffmann's 'taste' was thought suspect by the superior Speer. *The Haus der Deutschen Kunst* (House of German Art) was one of Hitler's favourite projects. It fitted his self-image as artist and connoisseur, patron of the arts, to replace Munich's art gallery (the 'Glass House', destroyed in a fire in 1931) with one of his own inspiration and design. The architect Hitler chose to execute his plan was Professor Paul Ludwig Troost, who had remodelled the Braun Haus and the new Chancellor's Berlin residence. Albert Speer, who was to succeed Troost, shared Hitler's admiration for his work. Troost's style was neo-classical – to Hitler *the* quintessential style. It is ironic that he came from the same artistic stable as Walter Gropius, whose Bauhaus Hitler closed.

A traumatic incident occurred when Hitler laid the ceremonial cornerstone of the gallery on 15 October 1933. The silver hammer, with which he laid the stone in place, shattered. The superstitious Hitler,

[55]

visibly shaken, took the breakage as a bad omen. He was convinced it had been so when Troost died three months later, on 21 January 1934.

The gallery was built in Prinzregentenstrasse and Hoffmann and the outspoken Frau Troost were among the chosen few who helped Hitler review the choices of the jury of twelve professors who selected the pictures to be hung. Tempers frayed and opinions varied, but the gallery opened on the due day, 18 July 1937.

Despite the influence of Hoffmann and Frau Troost, the majority of exhibits were in the vapid, stereotyped, wooden, romantic, idealised style that Hitler considered as art. Also included were sculptures by Arno Breker, Hitler's favourite sculptor. Breker, born in 1900, was still living in Dusseldorf in 1983, vainly trying to shake off the stigma of being the preferred sculptor of the Third Reich. As with Troost, it was Breker's neo-classicist, traditional representational style which appealed to Hitler. He had first admired Breker's 1935 statue of Dionysus, designed for the 1935 Olympic Games. The exhibition changed annually, but each year a portrait of Hitler was shown, which he himself selected. The most popular was Lanzinger's 'Hitler in Knight's Armour' one of the most reproduced of all the Führer's portraits, which was exhibited in 1938. Each year, to coincide with the new exhibition a *Tag der Deutschen Kunst* (Day of German Art) was celebrated, with the publication of commemorative postcards and stamps.

---

124. The house painter
War-time Allied propaganda picture of Hitler (or Schicklgruber) as a decorator rather than an artist. The pages of *Mein Kampf* hang for use as toilet paper. The lavatorial style of humour was much favoured by the Germans during the First World War.
American: Pub. Hilborn Novelty Cd., New York. Value B.

125 'Haus der Deutschen Kunst, München' (House of German Art, Munich)
A watercolour representation of Prof. Troost's building in Prinzregentenstrasse, by R. Geibel-Hellmeck.
German: Pub. M. Geidleim. No. 262. Value B.

The following are paintings which were selected to be exhibited in the House of German Art, and which exemplify the approved NSDAP, Hitler-inspired, concept of 'art'. 'HDK' is the abbreviation of *Haus der Deutschen Kunst*.

126. 'Vesper'
Lothar Sperle's ideal German peasant family. The mother suckles her blonde baby from her copious breasts, while the father slices the symbolic bread.
German: Pub Max Hirmer, for the NSDAP. Value B.

The following eleven postcards were all photographed and published by Hoffmann's Munich studios.
All are German: Value B.

127. 'Sitzende Blondine' (Seated Blonde)
Artist Wilhelm Hempfing. HDK No. 181.

128. 'Die Ruhende' (The Rest)
A tame version of Goya's 'La Maja Desnuda' by Johann Schult. HDK No. 284.

129. 'Die Sinne' (The Senses)
The five senses, somewhat woodenly portrayed by Ivo Saliger. HDK No. 194.

THE HOUSE PAINTER

124

125

126

127

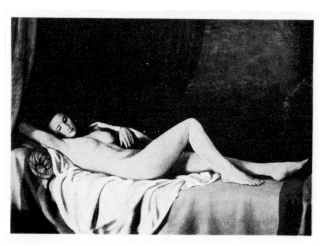

128

129

130

131

132

133

130. 'Kunst Und Naturfreund' (Art and Artlessness)
A spark of humour is evident in A. Reich's painting. HDK No. 143.
Colour illustration on page 75.

131. 'Bacchus and Ariadne'
Karl Truppe's Bacchus looks more like a domesticated Norseman on a Saturday night. Ariadne's poodle-like dog seems more alarmed than she does! HDK No. 444

132. 'Im Lebensfrühling' (In Life's Springtime)
Johann Schult's approved Teutonic maidens have a somewhat androidal air about them! HDK No. 411

133. 'Najade an der Quelle' (Naiad at the Spring)
Arnst Liebermann's standard transposition from Greek mythology to Aryan idealism. HDK No. 408.

134

135

136

137

134. 'Schlafende Diana' (Sleeping Diana)
By Math. Padua. In 1938 another of Padua's submissions to the House of German Art caused somewhat of a sensation. It was his erotic interpretation of 'Leda and the Swan', a theme which, surprisingly, Hitler found compulsive. Bormann, however, an inveterate lecher, actually bought Padua's version. HDK No. 520.

135. 'Jugend' (Youth)
NSDAP version, by Julius Mahainz. HDK No. 502.

136. 'Fruchtbarkeit' (Fruitfulness)
A worthy German theme by Rich. Heymann. HDK No. 526.

137. 'Alt Braunau'
Old Braunau, the Austrian border town on the River Inn, where Hitler was born. Friedrich Schutz chose a fairly safe subject for his drawing. HDK No. 432.

138

139

140

141

142

143

138–143. Six portraits by W. Willrich

Wolf Willrich had been appointed as one of the arbiters of 'degenerate' art, and his own work was above suspicion. His portraits show sturdy, sober, worthy, healthy German peasant types, of the kind found desirable by Darré (q.v.), Hitler's first Minister of Agriculture, and founder of the RUSHA (Service of Race and Settlement). Darré was alarmed at Germany's diminishing peasant population as industrialisation took over. 'The death of the peasant is the death of our people', he maintained. 'It is not merely bread which grows in furrows; it is also our men.' Willrich's series, *Deutscher Blutadel in Aller Welt* (Aristocracy of German Blood throughout the World) was the pictorial expression of Darré's concepts. The postcard reproductions were sold in aid of the VDA, *Volksbund für das Deutschtum im Ausland* (League of Ex-patriate Germans). His style is reminiscent, especially in the black and white sketches, of another approved German artist, Albrecht Dürer! Willrich's characteristic 'W' signature initial, entwined with the date of the portrait, is pseudo-runic in format – another concession to Teutonic ancestry.

These six portraits are all value B.

138. 'Altbauer aus dem Ries (Bayern)'
Old peasant from Ries (Bavaria) 1937. No. 36.

139. 'Hildegard Breiner'
On reverse, *Des Edlen ewiges Reich* (The thoroughbreds of the eternal State) 1938. No. 11.

140. 'Mädchen aus Bessarabien' (Girl from Bessarabia)
Bessarabia was one of those oft-disputed territories which broke away from Russia after the 1917 Revolution to join with Rumania, an alliance ratified by the Treaty of Paris, 1920. Stalin and Hitler both had territorial designs on it in 1939 and it was a subject of discussion prior to the signing of the Russo-German Pact, 1939.

141. 'Westfälische Bauerntochter'
Daughter of Westphalian Peasant. 1935. No. 13.

142. 'Niedersachsen-Mädel'
Lass from Lower Saxony. 1939. No. 15.

143. Förstersfrau aus dem Buchenland'
Forester's Wife from Buchenland. 1939.

It's That Man Again
1937-1939
▼━━━━━━━▼

By 1937 Hitler was supremely confident of his control over Germany – its people, its party and its soldiers. Not only had he built up his armed forces, but he had also tried them out in a war in Spain. Now he could use them to persuade others to give in to his territorial demands. Europe, generally, wanted peace. France had assumed a defensive attitude and sheltered herself mentally and physically behind the Maginot Line. Her politicians had calculated that if she were to enter another war, and lose as many men as in the First World War, then France would gradually disappear, because the birth rate would never again exceed the death rate.

Britain, the most powerful and influential of European nations, also wanted peace. Her security came from being an island and from her traditional position as a naval power and world financial centre. With the assumptive arrogance that came from decades of ruling an empire, her politicians assumed a leadership role in pan-European affairs. The man at the top was Prime Minister Neville Chamberlain. Thus, as Hitler and his resurgent Germany played an ever more visible role on the world stage, a confrontation between the two men and their philosophies became inevitable.

In 1936, Hitler's troops had marched into the Rhineland in defiance of the Versailles Treaty. Neither Britain nor France had taken any action, being more concerned with social unrest at home and Mussolini's activities in Ethiopia. As a result, Hitler had proof positive that he could obtain what he wanted by a show of strength. All he had to be certain of was how far he could push Britain and France before they would find the determination to oppose him.

The other main result of the failure of Britain and France to stop Hitler in the Rhineland was that their Allies – Czechoslovakia, Poland, Russia, Rumania and Yugoslavia – no longer felt able to trust them to come to their aid. Thus a confident, aggressive Führer faced a disarray of nations who looked hesitatingly towards Britain and Neville Chamberlain for leadership.

The pictures and captions in this chapter are carefully arranged in a sequence to show, almost in comic-strip style, how Hitler gained territory after territory, simply by threatening to go to war. Up to and including Munich he had the sympathy of the British on his side. So determined was Chamberlain to preserve peace, and so deep rooted was his desire to be its 'pilgrim', that he was prepared to concede almost anything to the Führer – even things that were not his to give, such as Czechoslovakia! In March 1938 Germany occupied Austrian South Tyrol. The move did not please Mussolini, who had long coveted the area, and he is reported to have exclaimed 'That damned German!' However, publicly he gave Hitler his wholehearted support so that the two military dictators presented a common front to the rest of the world. They were a powerful combination.

Flushed with this success, Hitler looked for the next, and decided to take over the strip of Czechoslovakia along Germany's border known as the Sudetenland. He threatened force, and Neville Chamberlain fulfilled his cherished role as the pilgrim of peace by flying to Munich, and early on the morning of 30

September, signing an Agreement that gave the Sudetenland to Hitler the next day! The Czechs were not even represented at the talks.

Chamberlain flew home saying, 'it is peace for our time', while Hitler professed that he had, 'nothing more to ask'. But the countdown to war had now begun. After Munich, Britain could no longer go along with German territorial ambitions. One more annexation would prove that Hitler was not to be trusted. Hitler was on a wave of success, and the nation was fed and fuelled by his achievements. It needed more, and with Hitler's 50th birthday coming up he was running out of time in which to complete the foundations of his 'Thousand Year Reich'. There was nowhere to go but forward.

On 15 March 1939 Germany invaded Bohemia and Moravia, the remaining heart of Czechoslovakia. On 23 March she occupied Memel and demanded that Danzig be given the right to choose whether it wished to become part of Greater Germany. But Hitler could not wait for political formalities. Everyone had given in before. Why not this time?

Early in the morning of 1 September 1939, German forces invaded Poland and occupied Danzig. Around midday Hitler faced the Reichstag and told them what had happened. That historic moment, the open declaration of what would become the Second World War, is captured by the last card in Part I of this book (card 190). Hitler had finally pushed too hard.

144

144. 'Exposition International Paris 1937'

Since before the turn of the century, national pride and tourism had been stimulated by international exhibitions. France, with regular events held in Paris, was well to the fore. The spectacular Eiffel Tower was the main attraction at the 1889 Exhibition and it was the opportunity to post a picture card from the top of the Tower that set alight the craze for collecting picture postcards during the early 1900s. The 1937 Paris Exhibition was concerned in particular with art and design. This card shows the German pavilion built specially for the event, and the heavy, epic style favoured by Hitler is very evident. In the cinema category Leni Riefenstahl's film of the 1934 Nuremberg Rally, 'Triumph of the Will', won a gold medal. Another gold medal was won by Albert Speer for his model of the Reichsparteitag area in Nuremberg, and yet another for his design of the German pavilion pictured here. Hitler had not liked the first design sketches which he had been shown and threatened to withdraw from the exhibition. Albert Speer chanced upon a drawing of the Soviet pavilion, which had two 10 m (35 ft) tall figures, apparently striding towards the Germans. He therefore designed the massive column as if to block the figures and placed a huge eagle on top to look down upon them. Hitler was pleased.

French: Pub. H. Chipault. No. 107. 1937. Value B.

145

146

147

148

145. Motorcycle racing, Stuttgart 1937

Every facet of German life was subordinated to the greater design of the party. The superiority of the Aryan race over all others was a cornerstone of NSDAP philosophy and therefore in any competitive field the Germans had to be seen to be the best. But in addition to the image-building effects of German victories, in events such as motorcycle racing, there was the resultant stimulus given to technological innovation. During the First World War, the motorcycle had been used for message carrying, traffic control, reconnaissance and for transport by machine-gun units. In 1938 the SS motorcycling team won the Donnington International 6 Day Trial and, when presented with the trophy cup, gave the Hitler salute. A loud raspberry floated over from the direction of the British team. German industry used the cover of international sport and commerce to hide their development of modern military automotive vehicles and aeroplanes.

German: Pub. German Post Office. 1937. Value B.

146, 147, 148. S.A. *Wettkämpfe*', Berlin 1937 (three cards)

These black and white cards commemorating the SA 'Games' from 13 to 15 August 1937 are typical examples of 'approved' German art. The style is simple, direct and powerful, echoing the drama of the SA uniforms and parades. At the very beginnings of the Nazi movement, when the SA role was essentially to keep order at Nazi political meetings, by brute force if need be, their disciplined street parades in the midst of street chaos gave many Germans a needed sense of security. The SA (*Sturmabteilung* – Storm Detachment) developed out of the right-wing Freikorps and volunteer units, when they were disbanded in 1921 under pressure from the Allies. At first, the organisation masqueraded as a 'Gymnastic and Sports Section', but was renamed the SA by its leader Ernst Röhm. The loyalty of the SA rank and file, however, was not given 100 per cent to Hitler, but often to their own Officers, and Hitler knew that many senior SA men would not hesitate to get rid of him if it suited them to do so.

His first step towards curtailing the independent power of the SA, was the appointment of his old friend Hermann Goering as their titular head in 1922, but that still did not guarantee his personal safety. As a result of the failure of the Munich putsch in 1923, when Hitler was sent to Landsberg prison, the authorities placed a temporary ban on the SA. In Hitler's absence Ernst Röhm strengthened his own executive hold over the fragmented organisation and seemed intent on going his own way. On 9 November 1925 in reaction, Hitler officially announced the formation of a special Protection Squad (*Schutzstaffel* – shortened to SS) whose sworn loyalty was to himself alone. It was to become the most powerful force in the Third Reich.

Although Röhm avowed loyalty to Hitler, relations between the SS and the SA became increasingly strained. The clique of homosexuals that administered the SA at the top, including Röhm, became ever overt in their activities, thus allowing the SS by comparison to assume an air of morality which was totally unjustified.

By 1934 there were over 4 million SA men throughout Germany with local leaders, particularly in Berlin, conducting a reign of terror almost at will. The restless aggression of the SA posed a threat to central constitutional government of the country, and political and military leaders began to speak out against it. To Hitler personally, Röhm appeared as a direct rival to his own leadership. It was time for drastic action, but Hitler hesitated.

Himmler, Head of the SS, and his second in command, Reinhard Heydrich (both subordinate to Röhm), with the full and active support of Goering, manufactured evidence that the SA were preparing an armed coup. Hitler was convinced, and acted. He summoned Röhm and all SA leaders to meet him at the Pension Hanselbauer at Bad Wiessel in Bavaria at 1100 hours on 30 June 1934. Sepp Dietrich, commander of the SS Liebstandarte Adolf Hitler, secretly assembled his men nearby. At 6 o'clock on the morning of 30 June 1934, Hitler stormed into the Pension, accused Röhm and the others of being traitors and ordered their arrest. They were bundled off to Stadelheim prison and there, later, were shot by Dietrich's men. Himmler and Heydrich began their own murders in Berlin, and the assassinations, dictated by lists made almost at whim by the SS, went on all over Germany. Practically anyone who had offended the SS in any way fell victim to the terror. Before the 'Night of the Long Knives' was over, Röhm and sixteen senior SA leaders were dead, but the total number killed will never be known. Some reports suggest that more than 500 people were murdered.

Up to this time the SS had been under the command of Röhm, head of the SA. On 20 July 1934 Hitler declared the SS an independent formation of the NSDAP. The men with the black cap and silver Death's Head badge, black jacket, black tie, black breeches and black boots were firmly on the road to power. The 'brown men' pictured here, the SA, though numbering tens of thousands, and impressively paraded and trained as at these 'Games' in 1937, were emasculated.

German: 1937 Artist F. Lecktner. Value C each card.

149

150

151

152

153

154

149–154. Six official postal stationery cards

The annual party rally at Nuremberg continued to develop as the central ceremonial event of the year. In 1937 the theme name chosen for it was 'Party Day of Work'. Although no new postage stamps were issued, a set of eight postal stationery cards, contained in a special envelope, was on sale. A percentage of the income from the cards (they cost 25 Rpf each) went to the 'Culture Fund'.

Six of the cards are illustrated. Each card Value B.

149.

SS standard bearers. The Romanesque design of the standards originated with Adolf Hitler.

150.

The *Reichsarbeitsdienst* (Labour Corps). Almost 40,000 uniformed men carrying their shovels performed their own ceremonial parade on 9 September.

151.

Party officials. The stamp printed on this card and the others is a design by Richard Klein, from a Heinrich Hoffmann photograph.

152.

Hitler (centre), Lutze (right) and Himmler, pay tribute to the dead in the Luitpold arena. The picture is from a Hoffmann photograph, taken at the 1934 'Triumph of the Will' Rally.

153.

Hitler believed that the future of Germany lay with its young people and therefore they must be taught the Nazi philosophy. Boys, like this one, between ten and fourteen, were enrolled in the *Jungvolk* (Young People) organisation which prepared them for entry into the Hitler Youth. On graduating from the Jungvolk, each boy was given a dagger upon which was engraved 'Blood and Honour'.

154.

The SA on the march. A popular marching song was 'When the SA and the SS March Out'. According to the words, everybody would be envious and all the girls impressed. This card was posted in Berlin on 14 September, 1937, the day after the rally ended. The message on the back reads:

> 'My dear Mother,
> Today you have another greeting from me. I didn't go to the office to-day as I did not feel well and have a bad headache. The day before yesterday I was in the Adolf Hitler Stadium. To-day I still have the aches and pains from it . . .'

155

155. 13 March 1938

'One People, One State, One Leader' is the slogan which encapsulated the Nazi ideal. Hitler *was* Germany and his aims were Germany's. An Austrian himself, he wanted to bring his homeland into the bosom of the country which he now ruled. After the First World War, Austria formed herself into an independent republic with nine states: Vienna, Tyrol, Lower Austria, Upper Austria, Burgenland, Styria, Salzburg, Carinthia and Vorarlberg. In 1934, Nazis in Vienna staged a coup, during which the Austrian Chancellor Dollfuss was murdered, and which might have succeeded if Italian forces had not moved up to the Brenner Pass in support of Austria. Kurt Schuschnigg then became Chancellor, and was soon forced to make concessions to Hitler, including the acceptance of the Nazis as a legal party in February 1938. Able to move openly, the Nazis began to cause unrest and disorder, and Hitler insisted that the Austrian people should be allowed to vote upon whether they wished to become part of Germany. Schuschnigg had no alternative but to agree, but before the vote was taken German troops marched into Austria on 12 March 1938, on the pretence of maintaining law and order. When the vote was taken it was overwhelmingly in Hitler's favour. German: Pub. Brendamour, Simbart and Co. 1938. Value B.

Ein Volk - Ein Reich - Ein Führer!

Ja!

10. 4. 38

156

Österreich kehrt heim!
10. April 1938

157

VOJÁCI DĚTEM

158

GAUTAG ESSEN
19 38

159

SA
Postkarte
Reichswettkämpfe
Berlin, 15.-17. Juli 1938

160

1 9 3 8
Deutsches Turn- und Sportfest
Breslau

161

156. One People, One State, One Leader, 10 April 1938

When Hitler and his forces marched into Austria in 'Operation Otto', they were welcomed by the mass of the population. Almost 1 million people were unemployed, and the prospect of uniting with a thriving Germany seemed a solution to that problem. Hitler, too, was excited by the event. Austria was his homeland and now he had brought it back into a Greater Germany. A nationwide Nazi-controlled plebiscite was held on 10 April 1938. Germans approved of the annexation because it was a step towards obtaining the *Lebensraum* (living space) that Hitler had led them to anticipate. Austrians saw Hitler as a saviour. This picture shows Greater Germany with East Prussia at the top separated by the Polish 'corridor'. Superimposed upon the map is a golden German eagle with the word *Ja!* (Yes!). The card was presumably a propaganda issue to encourage Germans to vote in Hitler's favour: 99 per cent did.

German: Adhesive stamps. Cancelled 10 April 1938. Value C.

Colour illustration on page 75.

157. 10 April 1938

A propaganda card encouraging Austrians to vote 'Yes' for union with Germany, this issue was posted in Vienna on 9 April 1938, a day which had been designated by the Nazis as 'Day of Greater Germany'. 'Greater Germany' was the name set aside for Germany *after* its absorption of Austria. The vote was due on 10 April, the day after this card was posted. The caption reads 'Austria comes home' and around the central swastika are the coats of arms of the nine Austrian states. Less than three weeks later, Hitler gave secret orders to General Keitel, setting out 'Operation Green' – the invasion of Czechoslovakia. The Nazi steamroller was on the move.

German: 1938. Value C.

Colour illustration on page 75.

158. 'Vojáci Dětem'

Part of Hitler's propaganda campaign to justify his aggressive actions against neighbouring territories, was to complain loudly about the mistreatment of German minorities in those countries. Complaints about Czechoslovakian oppression of Germans in the Sudetenland began in the early 1930s. When Hitler marched into Austria in March 1938, to the delight of the 8 million Germans there, the 3 million Germans in the Sudetenland began to agitate for their own union with Germany. Hitler called them 'these tortured creatures'. The Czechs under President Edward Benes ordered partial mobilisation. France followed suit in support of Poland. By September 1938 they had mobilised 1½ million soldiers between them to face any attempt by Hitler to invade Czech territory. War seemed imminent. This card welcomes Czech mobilisation in defence of their homeland. On the back is an adhesive stamp proclaiming Franco-Czech solidarity. It was posted on 29 May 1938. Four months later Neville Chamberlain was in Munich.

Czech: Pub. Czech authorities. 1938. Value D.

159. 'Gautag Essen' 1938

This is a splendid card in woven silk, very similar to the cards produced in Coventry by Thomas Stevens before the First World War. The word *Gau* means region or district. In this case the district is Essen. Thus this card celebrates Party Day in Essen. Each NSDAP region had its own leader, or *Leiter*, hence the word *Gauleiter* for local party officials.

German: Pub. Dr R. Morisse, Wuppertal. 1938. Value D.

Colour illustration on page 75.

160. 'SA Reichswettkämpfe'. Berlin, 15–17 July 1938

Although the independent power of the brownshirted SA had been purged in the 1934 'Night of the Long Knives', as the first and largest organised body of the NSDAP it played an important part in promoting Nazi ideals. The purge had 'cleansed' the SA of its more brutal elements, and thereafter emphasis was placed upon public displays of discipline, physical fitness and overwhelming numbers, in order to ensure co-operation of the populace. Morale within the SA was maintained by detailed ceremonial activities, merit badges, a clear promotion structure and regular gatherings such as this camp in Berlin. That same month, July 1938, General Ludwig Beck, Chief of Army Staff, resigned in protest against what he considered to be Hitler's preparations for war. He had hoped that all Germany's generals would resign with him. None did.

German: Pub. German Post Office. 1938. Value B.

161. 'Deutsches Turn-und Sportfest', Breslau 1938

Breslau is a town near Germany's 1938 eastern border with Poland, at the junction of the Oder and the Ohle rivers. Its historical connections with Poland are strong enough for it to have an alternative, Polish, name of Wrocław. The German nation by 1938 was very self-confident. The policies of the Nazis had put the people back to work, industry was booming, and the Führer had promised to return Germany to a prominent place in world affairs. These blond and muscular athletes are exchanging a relay baton, symbolising the teamwork between all facets of society, that NSDAP philosophies demanded. A show of Aryan strength near the border must have added to the envy of their homeland felt by German minorities living in Poland, and increased their desire to be part of Hitler's obvious success.

German: 1938. Pub. Anon. Cancelled 31 July 1938 in Breslau. Value C.

Colour illustration on page 75.

162

16.

164

Der große Appell im Luitpoldhain: Der Führer weiht neue Fahnen mit der Blutfahne   38/39

16.

166

162. 'Tag der Gemeinschaft'

This is a view of the Zeppelin Field in Nuremberg on 8 September 1938 during the 10th Party Rally. Each of the days of the rally, which ran from 5 to 12 September, had its own name. On this day, 'Community Day', there were mass displays of gymnastics and team exercises. At around midnight the following day, Hitler secretly met Keitel in the Deutscher Hof Hotel in Nuremberg in order to finalise 'Operation Green', the plan for the invasion of Czechoslovakia. All of Europe, still on edge after the German absorption of Austria and fearful of the armed, if static, confrontation between Germany, France, and Czechoslovakia, waited breathlessly for the last day of the rally when, traditionally, the Führer gave his main speech. What would he say?

German: Pub. Intra. Nuremberg. 1938. Value C.

163. The Luitpold arena

These three montage views show the Luitpold arena as it was in September 1938. Originally a park laid out for the Bavarian Jubilee Exhibition of 1906, it was developed as a ceremonial complex by the NSDAP. It was here that the party units such as the SS, the SA and the NSKK (National Socialist Motor Corps) held their rallies. At one side was the First World War memorial erected by the citizens of Nuremberg between 1928 and 1930, and immediately opposite on the other, a large rectangular tribune flanked by spectators' seating, put up by the Nazis between 1935 and 1937. The card shows the central tribune topped by three swastikas. It was here that Hitler stood to review 150,000 SA and SS men on 11 September 1938, four days before meeting the British Prime Minister Neville Chamberlain at Berchtesgaden to discuss Czechoslovakia. The huge bronze eagles stood on pillars at either end of the tribune.

German: Pub. Ludwig. Riffelmacher. 1938. Value C.

164. Hitler with the Blood Flag

Two public Nazi ceremonies in particular were conducted in a manner akin to religious ceremonies. One was the annual parade at the Feldherrnhalle on 9 November, when the sixteen martyrs of the Munich putsch were remembered with reenactment, and torch-lit oath-taking. The second was the one pictured here – the consecration of a new SA or SS standard. Each new colour or standard was reverently touched by the *Blutfahne* (Blood Flag) symbolising the passing to the new unit of the spirit and commitment of those who died at Munich in 1923. The Blutfahne was the flag they carried and was supposedly covered in their blood. Hitler performed the ceremony in the style of some ancient priest performing a holy rite, holding the Blutfahne in one hand and the new colour in the other so that the mystical essence ran through his body.

German: Pub. Zerruss and Co. Nuremberg. *Circa* 1937. Posted 14 September. 1938. Value C.

165. Masaryk and Běnes

On the left is Jan Masaryk and on the right Edvard Běnes. In 1938, Masaryk, a previous Slovak President, was Czech Ambassador to Germany, while Běnes was President of Czechoslovakia. Their country was made up of a mix of dissatisfied minority groups, the most difficult of which were the 3 million Germans in the Sudetenland, a strip of highly industrialised land in western Bohemia (a Czech province) along the German border. Hitler's designs upon the Sudetenland were clear to all and the German minority through their Sudeten German Party made their wish to join Germany very clear. Hitler's speech on the last day of the 1938 'Greater Germany' Rally (named in honour of the Greater Germany formed by the absorption of Austria barely six months earlier) was nervously awaited by Masaryk and Běnes and by the statesmen of Europe. To their surprise, the Führer, though he roundly condemned the Czechs for supposed ill-treatment of the German minority, gave no ultimatum. In their relief they began to believe that a negotiated solution to the problem was possible. What they did not know was that three days before Hitler had finalised the plan for the invasion of Czechoslovakia.

Czech: Pub. Neubert. *Circa* 1937. Value B.

166. 'Asch ist frei! Heil Hitler!'

The relief felt by the Czechs, British and French as a result of the absence of an ultimatum in Hitler's speech at Nuremberg on 12 September, was short lived. The Sudeten Germans, fired by the Führer's oratory, rioted in the streets. Prime Minister Daladier of France, fearing a German armed intervention, appealed to Britain for help. British Prime Minister Neville Chamberlain flew to Germany and met Hitler at Berchtesgaden on 16 September. Hitler demanded that the Sudeten Germans should be given the right to choose for themselves which country they would belong to. Chamberlain returned to London for discussions with the French and the Czechs. Five days later on 21 September he returned to Germany and met the Führer at Bad Godesberg on the Rhine. He was prepared to agree to Hitler's demands. But Hitler now wanted immediate occupation of the Sudetenland, and as they spoke, news arrived that German troops had crossed the Czech Frontier at Asch in reaction to 'border incidents', and that twelve German hostages had been shot. Chamberlain flew home and called an emergency meeting of the Cabinet. Six days later he met Hitler again at Munich where the 'Agreement' for peace was signed. This card celebrates the German occupation of Asch on 21 September 1938 — 'Asch is free! Heil Hitler!' It was posted in Asch on 23 September. Either a designer and printer worked overtime to produce it, or someone prepared the design and printed the card before the event! Or did the postman backdate his cancellation?

German: Pub. anon. 1938. Value D.

THE PILGRIM OF PEACE
BRAVO! MR. CHAMBERLAIN

167

168

DRUHÝ PRESIDENT
REPUBLIKY ČESKOSLOVENSKÉ
DR. EDVARD BENEŠ.

169

167. The pilgrim of peace

'Bravo! Mr Chamberlain', says the by-line to this caption. Most people in Europe wanted peace and that included the British. Traditionally the British held the French rather than the Germans to be their enemies, and there was considerable sympathy for Germany's wish to bring under its protective control the ex-patriate minorities separated from it by the terms of the Versailles Treaty. Chamberlain, who became Prime Minister in May 1937, took a very personal interest in the maintenance of peace by diplomacy, a policy that became known as 'appeasement'. This picture, almost certainly taken early in September 1938, shows the Prime Minister in the confident mood that he must have felt on his way to Bad Godesberg on 21 September, when he thought that he had solved the Czech crisis – or when he flew back to England on 30 September thinking that he had (again?) solved the crisis. In both cases he was wrong. British: Pub. Tuck. 1938. Value B.

168. Hitler and Chamberlain

In September 1938, in an attempt to prevent a war over Germany's determination to unite with Czechoslovakian Sudetenland, Chamberlain flew to see Hitler three times. The second visit was in order to give in to the demands that the Führer had made at their first meeting. The third visit, (to Munich), was in order to give in to the demands that Hitler had made at their second meeting. When Chamberlain landed at Heston Airport near Croydon on 30 September he waved the Agreement which had been signed in Munich and said 'I've got it!' and later in London uttered the words that he lived to regret 'I believe it is peace for our time'.
German. Pub. anon. 1938. Value B.

169. Dr Edvard Běnes, President of Czechoslovakia

In order to pacify Hitler, Běnes had agreed, under pressure from Britain and France, to allow a plebiscite to be held in the Sudetenland. But by the time Chamberlain took the message to Hitler on 21 September the Führer was about to march into Czechoslovakia. In a last-ditch attempt to maintain peace, Chamberlain and Daladier, the French Prime Minister, went to meet Hitler at Munich on 29 September 1938. They were prepared to dismember Czechoslovakia and give her to Hitler if that was the only way to preserve the peace. The most notable absentee at Munich was Edvard Běnes, the man whose country was to be sacrificed.
Czech: Pub. anon. *Circa* 1937. Value B.

20

40

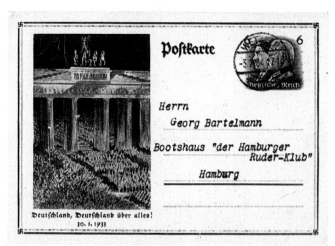

59

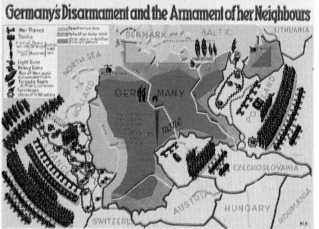

60

62

67

81

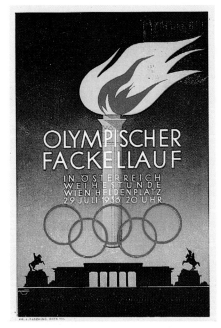

89

93

109

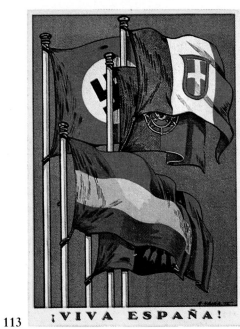

113

115

121

130

156

157

159

161

Und Ihr habt doch gesiegt!

178

179

DANZIG IST DEUTSCH

189

198

247

254

170

171

172

170. Mussolini and Hitler at Kufstein

The card carries the caption, 'The meeting', and the excitement that the two dictators felt as they met is very clear. Chamberlain had appealed to Mussolini to persuade his friend Hitler not to go to war over the Sudetenland, and Mussolini had suggested a meeting in Munich. Hitler, however, needed Mussolini openly to support Germany so that Britain and France would not feel able to resist his plans. On 28 September, the day before Munich, Mussolini sent Hitler a message – 'Whatever you decide Führer, Fascist Italy stands behind you'. At 6 p.m. that evening Il Duce left Rome in his special train, seen off by cheering crowds, and was met early on the 29 September by Hitler at the small town of Kufstein near the Austrian border, not far from Munich. The moment of their first handshake, captured in this remarkable postcard, must have been an electric one for both of them. Fellow conspirators, they were off to play political poker against Britain and France. In the pot was Czechoslovakia.

Italian: Pub. Fotorapida. Rome. 1938. Value D.

171. A poker four

This photomontage of the principal characters in the Munich drama shows them playing poker. It is a shrewd and accurate observation from neutral Switzerland of what happened. The hands held by the players can be made out using a magnifying glass. Daladier has shown his hand with the air of a participant rather than a winner. He has a full house, jacks on queens. Chamberlain obviously confident that things are going his way, has also exposed his hand. He has a straight flush, queen high, and so beats Daladier. Mussolini however has not declared his hand. He has four kings and so beats Chamberlain and Daladier. Hitler, totally relaxed, has certainly not let anyone know what his hand is. He is allowing Daladier and Chamberlain to have their brief moment of glory, but he controls the game – he has four aces.

Swiss: Pub. Lilian Lausanne. 1938. Value C.

172. Signing the Munich Agreement

The principals and their aides assembled in a room overlooking the Koenig's Platz in Munich, shortly after midday on 29 September. As no chairman had been nominated, Mussolini gradually assumed a co-ordinating role, since he could speak all the languages involved – Italian, German, French and English. Discussions went on all afternoon and into the evening, and it was not until the small hours of 30 September that an agreed document was produced. Hitler got everything he wanted. The evacuation of the Czechs from the Sudetenland was to begin the following day, 1 October. Here Daladier is signing the Agreement.

German: Pub. Hoffmann. No. S 10/4. 1938. Value C.

Zur historischen Begegnung   29. Septbr. 1938 in München

173

174

175

WIR DANKEN UNSERM FÜHRER

176

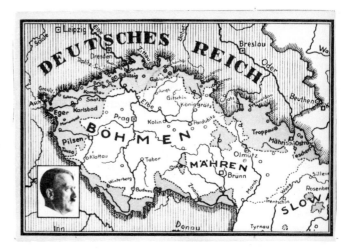

177

Und Ihr habt doch gesiegt!

178

175. Hitler and Co.

The Führer's entourage at Munich was considerable. This group, left to right, is Goering, Mussolini, Hess, Hitler and Count Galeazzo Ciano, Italian Foreign Minister and Il Duce's son-in-law. It was Ciano who maintained the link between the two dictators and who had conducted the negotiations in 1936 which had established the Axis. During the First World War, when causes and personalities became closely identified with one another, leading politicians and soldiers became known as 'Men of the Hour'. The caption on the reverse of this card is 'Men of the Hour'.

German: Pub. Huber, Munich. No. 125. 1938. Value C.

176. 'Wir danken unserm Führer'

The card shows Hitler and Co. girdled by the almost circular strip of Czechoslovakia known as the Sudetenland. Czech territory pushed into Germany, much as a gloved thumb would push into soft putty. The thin glove between thumb and putty was the Sudetenland, and on the map the most westerly Sudeten town next to the German border is Asch. Hitler wanted the Sudetenland. Benes intended to keep it, but lacking support from Britain and France he could not. On 29 September at Munich, the Sudeten strip was handed over to Hitler, and the German people expressed their feelings as in this card. 'We thank our Führer'.

German: Pub. Simpart, Munich. 1938. Value B.

177. 'Deutsches Reich Böhmen'

Another card celebrating the absorption by Germany of the Sudetenland, the map clearly shows how the territory lay between Böhmen (Bohemia) and Germany. At Munich, Hitler was 'given' the territory by the French and the British. Czech evacuation was to begin on 1 October. This card was issued on 1 October 1938.

German: Pub. W. Nolting, Hamburg. 1938. Value C.

178. 'Und Ihr habt doch gesiegt!'

The Nazi calendar was studded with 'special' days. This 'official remembrance card' for 9 November 1938, the 15th anniversary of the Munich putsch, has a title which freely translated means 'Despite all, you have won!' It certainly was a special day to remember in 1938, because that year Hitler had occupied Austria and Sudetenland, and had fooled Chamberlain and Daladier at Munich. The drawing has the Feldherrnhalle building in the background and the figures are standing near to where, fifteen years earlier, the Nazi martyrs had been shot down. The NSDAP, Hitler and Germany, had come a long way.

German: Pub. Bruckmann, Munich. 1938. Cancelled 9.11.38. Artist E. Ebor. Value D.

Colour illustration on page 76.

174. Hitler and Co. at Munich

This group were probably photographed at about 02.00 hours on 30 September 1938, just after the signing of the Munich Agreement. Chamberlain and Daladier on the left look dismayed. Well they might, because their next task was to explain to the waiting Czech emissaries what had happened to their country. Hitler, Mussolini and at the end, Ciano, Il Duce's son-in-law, don't seem any happier.

They were better poker players! The card is an interesting commemorative item. The title on the reverse is 'Historic Four Power World Conference in Munich 29 September 1938'. There is a Czech stamp which is cancelled with a 21 September date (the date that German troops marched into Asch), and the Nazi eagle and swastika crowning the words 'We have borne the yoke. Now we are free and remain free.'

German: Pub. Hoffmann. 1938. Value C.

173. Chamberlain, Daladier, Mussolini and Hitler

This is a double card consisting of two normal cards joined together, rather in the manner of a reply-paid postcard. It was issued to commemorate 'The Historic Negotiations, 29 September 1938 in Munich', and has been franked via a philatelic bureau with the date 9 November 1938, the 15th anniversary of the Munich putsch. Chamberlain was not known for his smile but the Germans seem to have caught him in a good humour.

German: Pub. O. Struck. Berlin. 1938. Value C.

179

180

Internat. Automobil- u. Motorrad-Ausstellung Berlin 1939

181

18

183

184

179. 'Ein Volk – Ein Reich – Ein Führer'

One people, one country, one leader – as 1938 came to an end, Germany was riding high. Her leader was fulfilling his promises. The nation was proud and excited, unemployment was under control and one by one the Führer was bringing back into *Grossdeutschland* (Greater Germany) the territories taken away by the Treaty of Versailles. This card celebrates that situation and commemorates the home-coming ('*Heimkehr*') of the Saar (1.3.35), Austria (12.3.38) and the Sudetenland (1.10.38). At the top right-hand corner is an isolated piece of Germany, East Prussia, and between her and her homeland is a corridor of Polish territory. Now the Führer's eyes turned that way.

German: Pub. Otto Hoppe, Berlin. 1938. Value C.
Colour illustration on page 76.

180. Hitler with German girls

The day before the Ides of March 1939, German troops entered Prague. Less than a fortnight later they entered Memel on the East Prussian/Lithuanian border. Secretly, Hitler had already prepared for Operation White, the invasion of Poland, and had even set the date – 26 August 1939. To the overwhelming majority of Germans, Hitler was a Saviour, and could do no wrong. His aggressive blustering had, time after time, won territorial victories without having to go to war. Here he is pictured for his 50th birthday, 20 April 1939, probably in Braunau where he was born. The admiration, even adoration, on the faces of the young girls is very clear. His next chronological adventure would be into Poland, and that would ask for even greater commitment from the German nation.

German: Pub. German Post Office. Posted in Braunau, 29 April 1939. Value B.

181. The Volkswagen

Hitler had driven his country towards war right from his first association with the embryo German Workers' Party in 1919. Even the massive civil engineering projects which he had begun, such as the autobahn network, had not only a contribution to make towards curing unemployment, but also to military strategy. In the all-embracing aura of NSDAP superiority and prosperity that developed as Hitler strode from one international success to another, the people were promised by their leader the fulfilment of a dream held by the people of most industrialised countries – that each family would have its own motor car. The people's car (the Volkswagen) was designed by Professor Porsche and offered for sale at an extremely attractive price. Potential buyers were able to pay in instalments before delivery. NSDAP coffers did very well out of the arrangement, though not a single car was actually delivered for peaceful use. This model was enticingly displayed at the Berlin Motor Show.

German: Pub. Menzendorf. 1939. Value C.

182, 183, 184. Annexation of the Carpatho-Ukraine (three cards)

These three cards dramatically illustrate the value of the postcard as a photographic record that may not have survived in any other form. Simply because these pictures were published as postcards, they were placed in a postcard album and therefore protected and saved. The pictures were taken on 15 March 1939. During the Czech crisis of September 1938, Hungary had supported Germany, and as a 'reward' on 14 March 1939 had gained from Czechoslovakian control parts of Ruthenia, a small country bordering on Poland and Rumania. Father Voloshyn, head of the Ruthenian Government, declared what was left of his country to be independent and renamed it Carpatho-Ukraine. Twenty-four hours later, with German co-operation, Hungarian troops occupied Carpatho-Ukraine. These pictures record the meeting between German and Hungarian forces on the day of annexation. The photographer was certainly very quick off the mark in producing the postcards. One, posted to London on 27 March, was sent from the Hungarian capital with the following message: 'Received your letter today. I could manage Tues. or Wed. Holy Week, but perhaps the situation will have cleared one way or the other by the end of May. Everyone here advises waiting till then as now it is cold and rainy. However, if that is difficult for you and you prefer to *come now* answer *by return post* – perhaps air or telegram. Better a definite decision. Opinion here G [i.e. Germany] will not come in; can get all she wants without doing so. Love. N.C.' N.C. was as confused as all the statesmen of Europe. Hitler was not any longer concerned just with getting his way peacefully, his mind was set on war.

Each card Hungarian: Pub. Magyar Film. Budapest. 1939. Value C.

185

186

187

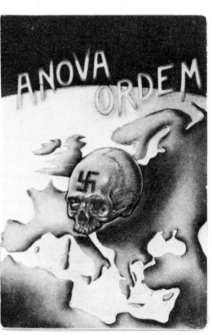

188

189

185. Hitler, 1889–1939

This card, issued to commemorate Hitler's 50th birthday on 20 April 1939, summarised his achievements to that time. As it turned out, the card also summarised what the Führer managed to do without causing a world war. His next 'achievement' in September, was the invasion of Poland. Among the listing here are:

'Saar 1935
Occupation of the Rhineland 1936
Integration of Austria March 1938
Integration of Sudetenland Sept. 1938
State protection of Bohemia and Moravia March 1939
Homecoming of Memel March 1939'

190

Few people outside of Germany saw the Führer's achievements in a similar vein of approval. Even those who had had sympathy for Germany because of the punishments imposed at Versailles, changed their minds at the beginning of 1939, when Hitler began to violate the Munich Agreement.
German: Pub. Hoffmann. 1939. Value C.
Colour illustration on the cover.

186. I've nothing more to ask
The French, more than any other nation, had been responsible for the heavy punishment meted out to Germany at the end of the First World War. They, unlike other European nations, had, therefore, little sympathy for Hitler's attempts to undermine the Versailles Treaty. As each annexation took place, Hitler avowed, 'I've nothing more to ask', and then proceeded on to his next objective. This French card, printed in English, in the hope of convincing Britain that Hitler could not be trusted, was accurately prophetic if published before 1 September 1939, when Hitler invaded Poland.
French: Pub. P.C. No. G20. 1939. Value C.

187. It's that man again
Comparable to the French, 'I've nothing more to ask' card, is this one, with the popular 1939 catchphrase, 'It's that man again'. The reference is to Hitler as he annexed yet another territory. On 12 July 1939 was the first broadcast of the radio show, 'ITMA', whose name is made up from the initial letters of the catch phrase. Written by Ted Kavanagh, produced by Francis Worsley, with a catchy signature tune by Michael North, it starred the comic genius, Tommy Handley. This card is one of a whole series featuring the catch phrases for which the show became famous.
British: Pub. Tuck. *Circa* 1939. Artist Bert Thomas. Value B.

188. 'A Nova Ordem'
This is a telling Portuguese prophesy of things to come. 'The New Order' reads the caption. At the outbreak of the Spanish Civil War, Portugal sided with Franco's Fascists, but later assumed a neutral position in relations with Spain and Nazi Germany. In reality, she sided with Britain and much anti-Nazi propaganda was distributed from Lisbon.
Portuguese: Pub. Anon. *Circa* 1939. Value D.

189. 'Danzig ist Deutsch'
'Danzig is German', were the words spoken by Hitler to greet the Foreign Minister of Poland, Josef Beck, when he came to Berchtesgaden to see him on 5 January 1939. The phrase had been used for several years as a slogan by the Nazi group among the city's politicians. Danzig had been established as a free city-port under the Versailles Treaty, and lay at the Baltic Sea end of the corridor of Poland which separated East Prussia from Germany. Once Hitler had regained the Sudetenland, and marched into Prague and Memel, Danzig was the next natural target. On 1 September 1939 German forces invaded Poland. Danzig was taken that day and formally proclaimed part of the Third Reich.
German: Pub. NSDAP, Munich. *Circa* 1939. Value C.
Colour illustration on page 76.

190. Hitler, 1 September 1939
This is a remarkable postcard, because it pictures Hitler at the moment that he was announcing to the German Parliament (Reichstag) that German forces had invaded Poland. Captured by the camera of Heinrich Hoffmann is the precise beginning of the Second World War. At just before 05.00 hours on Friday 1 September 1939, the German attack had begun, and 5 hours later Hitler stood before Parliament in Berlin's Kroll Opera House and told the Assembly what had happened. Listening to him were all of the capital's foreign correspondents, and short-wave radio broadcast a simultaneous commentary upon his speech around the world. It was twenty years earlier almost to the day, that the young Corporal Hitler had attended a meeting of the small German Workers' Party in a Munich beer cellar. Since then, by imagination, hard work, fanatical energy, murder, intrigue and an extraordinary sense of political balance, he had repudiated the terms of the Versailles Treaty, and dragged his country out of a depression into a prominent and proud position in world affairs. But this time he had miscalculated. Britain and France *would* go to war to defend Poland. Appeasement was dead, and what Hitler had taken twenty years to build would be destroyed in little more than a quarter of that time.
German: Pub. Hoffmann. No. P.1. September 1939. Value D.

Part Two

Dramatis personae

Part one of *Germany Awake!* examined the causes for, and development of, the NSDAP and its Axis Allies, up to the outbreak of the Second World War in September 1939. Part two profiles a selection of the main characters in the drama of those early years of the Nazi Party. Some of these were architects of its policy and its conduct – oversize, larger than life personalities, who vied with Hitler himself in their very outrageousness – like Goering, Goebbels, Hess, Röhm, Streicher. . . . Others were professional soldiers who, in their relief at finding in Hitler someone who had restored Germany's pride and self-confidence after the humiliations of Versailles, in many cases turned a blind eye to the immorality and ruthlessness of the régime. Among these were the soldiers who would become Hitler's generals: men like von Rundstedt, Keitel, von Manstein, von Kleist, Kesselring, Guderian, Rommel . . . sailors like Raeder, Dönitz, Lutzow . . . airmen like Student, Udet, von Richthofen, Molders. Others had particular talents that Hitler recognized and exploited: Dr Todt, whose 'organisation' was to set the foundations for massive building projects like the West Wall and the Atlantic Wall, or Otto Skorzeny, an early party member, whose daring eccentricity was to provide some of the most sensational exploits of the Second World War.

Then there were Hitler's Fascist allies: Mussolini, his early mentor and example, whose flamboyant régime was the pattern for the dramatic décor of the Nazi rallies; and some of Mussolini's aristocratic generals, like Umberto of Savoy and the Duke of Aosta. Hitler used the Spanish Civil War as a grand military exercise for his fledgling air force and growing army. Franco rewarded him by maintaining a shaky neutrality during the Second World War. Here we look at Franco and some of the men who helped him to shape Spain's destiny: General Mola and General de Llano.

In Part two the story of these personalities, who not only helped Hitler to establish the Third Reich, but who in many cases, remained with him to see its demise, is carried forward beyond the scope of Part One of this book.

But besides the policy-makers and the generals, the ordinary Germans in the street are featured. These are the men who, swept up by the contagious fanaticism that Hitler engendered, became his soldiers, sailors and airmen, ready to die for him as they often did. Indeed the two final portraits in the book are 'In Memoriam' cards.

Part two starts, however, with a profile of the man who virtually became Hitler's 'court photographer', Heinrich Hoffmann. His superb photographs provided a unique record, both of the growth of the party, its meetings and its dramatis personae, and of the wartime heroes of the three armed services and their achievements.

191

191. Heinrich Hoffmann

Heinrich Hoffmann was born in Bavaria in 1884, where his father was court photographer to the Prince Regent, Luitpold of Bavaria and others of the Royal Family. The young Heinrich entered the family business as an apprentice, and in 1900 he went to work in Darmstadt for the court photographer to the Grand Duke of Hesse. The position involved frequent visits to the ducal palace to photograph visiting royalty, like the Tsarina of Russia and Princess Louis of Battenburg. In search of new experiences, Hoffmann moved to Heidelberg (where he specialised in students' duels) and then to Frankfurt (where he concentrated on military photography). His next post (in 1903) was with another court photographer, this time an 'imperial' one in Hamburg. Here he photographed the King of Siam, a paralytically drunken Grand Duke of Russia, the Kaiser Wilhelm II and his uncle, Edward VII of England. The restless Hoffmann moved on to Switzerland, back to Munich and in 1907, to England, where he worked for the famous photographer, E. O. Hoppé. After two years of invaluable experience in the portrait field, Hoffmann returned to Munich. Caruso, Bruno Walther, Richard Strauss and again, the Kaiser, were among his subjects.

When the First World War broke out, Hoffmann was appointed as one of seven war photographers. One of his most interesting assignments was to photograph Roger Casement, the Irish traitor.

Returning to his native Munich after the war, Hoffmann recorded, and lucratively sold, pictures of the succession of political demonstrations, marches and mass meetings that took place there. During this period (in April 1920) Hoffmann joined a new political party – the Nazi Party – and was member No. 427.

In October 1922 an American photographic agency cabled him: 'send immediately photo adolf hitler offer hundred dollars'. So began an association with Hitler that was to last until their last meeting, in Berlin in April 1945, a few days before Hitler's death.

In 1922, Hitler, whose face in the next twenty-three years was to blazon forth around the world – on stamps, postcards, posters, in books, magazines and films, was deliberately avoiding being photographed as part of his carefully planned political campaign. Hoffmann's first attempt was thwarted when his camera was roughly confiscated by Himmler, but he went on to meet Hitler personally and to gain his confidence.

Hoffmann illicitly photographed Hitler's trial after the 1923 putsch, he snapped Hitler in Landsberg prison – again with a smuggled camera – and also took the famous photograph of the future Führer ostensibly leaving the prison. In actual fact, the prison authorities forbade any photographs and Hoffmann took the picture by the old city gates.

Their personal relationship developed as Hitler's authority grew, and as Hoffmann's business grew quite independently. When in Berlin they both occupied the Kaiserhof Hotel and Hoffmann was included by Hitler in many historic events. He refused, however, Goebbel's insistent offer that he should join the Propaganda Ministry; nor would he wear the special armband Goebbels had designed for all authorised press photographers.

When Hitler became Chancellor, Hoffmann photographed many of the foreign dignitaries and personalities who came to visit him, including Lloyd George (whom Hitler particularly admired), Anthony Eden, Oswald Mosley, Unity Mitford, Charles Lindbergh, King Boris of Bulgaria, King Michael of Rumania, and the Duke and Duchess of Windsor, on their controversial visit to Berchtesgaden. He also went to London to record the Coronation of King George VI in 1937.

When Hitler opened the House of German Art (q.v.) in Munich, he took the opportunity of making Hoffmann an honorary professor. He also took his friend and photographer with him on his triumphant entry into Austria in March 1938 and to the meeting with Mussolini, Chamberlain and Daladier in Munich. Hoffmann's photographs of these historic events and the principal players involved in them, were reproduced around the world.

The results of Hoffmann's epoch-changing travels with Hitler were often published in book form, e.g. 'With Hitler in Italy' (May 1938); 'With Hitler in Bohemia and Moravia' (March 1939); 'With Hitler in Poland' (September 1939). Copies of these books are collector's items today, but rarely crop up.

Hitler even sent Hoffmann to Moscow as his Special Envoy to report back on his impressions of Stalin and to photograph him signing the controversial German–Russian Pact of 23 August 1939.

Hitler, a confirmed non-smoker, insisted that Hoffmann blanked out Stalin's cigarette, while Stalin had forbidden publication of any photographs showing him drinking!

192

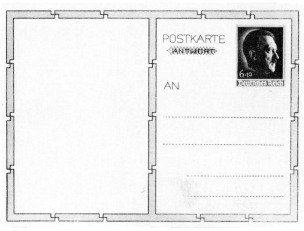

193

Having 'snapped' Mussolini and Stalin, Hoffmann was anxious to complete the trio of dictators by photographing Franco. Although he never travelled to Spain, Hoffmann's ambition was fulfilled when he met Franco and his son-in-law in France in October 1940.

Hoffmann regarded his relationship with Hitler as a personal one, rather than that of political/State leader and employee/official photographer. Certainly Hitler was relaxed in his company, and often casually asked his opinion. It was to Hoffmann that Hitler turned in his grief at the tragic death of his niece, Geli Raubal, generally accepted now as his only true love. And it was in Hoffmann's studio in 1930 that Hitler met Eva Braun, then working as a salesgirl, the woman who was to be his constant companion for the rest of his life, and his 'last minute' wife.

Hoffmann himself was not particularly interested in politics, nor was he an active party member, although Hitler awarded him the Special Gold Party Insignia (which he is wearing in the photograph illustrated here). A special rider was added to Hoffmann's 1948 appeal against his sentence by the Allies of ten years in a labour camp, that this special award, his professorship and his title of Official Photographer, should not be regarded as incriminating. He was finally released on 4 February 1950. Baldur von Schirach (his son-in-law) received a sentence of twenty years and Hoffmann's daughter, Henriette, divorced him.

During the fluctuating fortunes of the Second World War, Hoffmann continued to be Hitler's confidant and frequent house-companion at Obersalzberg and other of Hitler's headquarters. He accompanied his triumphant Führer to Compiègne to witness the humiliating defeat of France, in 1940. He recorded for posterity a succession of conquering generals, of Iron Cross winners. He photo-

graphed the shattered room in which the abortive attempt to blow Hitler up in July 1944, took place, and recorded Hitler in the ruins of Berlin in 1945. But throughout all the vicissitudes of the régime, of Hitler's own sometimes uncomfortable idiosyncracies, Hoffmann remained loyal to the man he called 'my friend'.

German: Pub. and photographed Hoffmann Studios, Berlin. Caption on reverse: 'Heinrich Hoffmann, the man, through whom the Führer sees. Official photographer of the Nazi party.

"Hitler, as he is little known" (Reichsmark 2.85) 250,000 copies.

"The Brown Forces" (Reichsmark 2.85) 60,000 copies.

"Hitler Youth" (Reichsmark 2.85) 60,000 copies.

"The Triumph of the Will" (Reichsmark 0.50) 300,000 copies.' Value D.

192, 193. Adolf Hitler

No publisher or photographer is named on this dramatically lit portrait of Hitler, although the picture was probably taken by Hoffmann, Hitler's personal photographer.

Bordered by a stylised swastika design, on the reverse as well as the front, the postcard is the 'answer' part of a reply-paid postcard. It bears the printed Richard Klein stamp, based on a profile portrait by Hoffmann designed for Hitler's birthday, and which was later overprinted 'Reichsparteitag 1938' for use at the Nuremberg Rally. The stamp is a 6 RPf denomination with a 19 RPf premium which went to Hitler's Culture Fund.

German: (Official card) 1938. Value D.

194   **195**   **196**

194. Adolf Hitler

This card was issued for the 1938 'Party Day of Greater Germany', which celebrated the acquisition of Austria. It carries a hand stamp (translated) 'Historic meeting, Chamberlain – Hitler'. The card has been posted twice: the first time at Nuremberg on the last day of the rally, 12 September, when Hitler threatened to use force against Czechoslovakia, and the second time at Berchtesgaden on 15 September, the day that Chamberlain flew there to meet Hitler for the first time.

German: Pub. J.E. Huber, No. 91 'Männer der Zeit' series. September 1938. Value D.

195. Adolf Hitler, Germany's Leader and Saviour

Another portrait taken during the visit to Vienna in 1938. Postally used on 16 March, it is franked *Der Führer in Wien*. On his left breast pocket, Hitler is wearing the Iron Cross First Class, awarded to him on 4 August 1918 by Lt Colonel von Tabeuf, on the recommendation of his Adjutant, Hugo Gutmann. The citation for the award reads: 'As a messenger he [Hitler], during both the static and mobile periods of warfare, exhibited exemplary conduct, cold-blooded courage, always volunteering to carry messages in the most difficult situations and under conditions of the greatest danger. After the destruction of all communications in difficult tactical conditions, it was the value of his indefatigable and unselfish actions that important messages were transmitted in spite of all difficulties.' Hitler had been promised the award by Gutmann if he volunteered to carry a message through particularly dangerous conditions. His successful delivery of the message to the German Artillery prevented the bombardment of their own infantry.

There is no disputing Hitler's bravery as a soldier. German: Pub. anon. 1938. Value C.

196. Reichskanzler Adolf Hitler

Another birthday portrait of the Chancellor. There are two postmarks on the reverse, one of Wien (Vienna), the other of Braunau (Hitler's birthplace). Both state: *20 April 1938. Des Führers Geburtstag.* Hitler's best birthday present that year was the result of the elections held on 9 April. In Germany, 99.02 per cent of the electorate voted in favour of *Anschluss* – the reunification of Austria with Germany – while in Austria 99.73 per cent voted for it. 'This is the proudest hour of my life', commented the Führer on this virtually unanimous vote of confidence.

German: Pub. Hoffmann. 1938. Value C.

197. Adolf Hitler

This picture of a contented and confident-looking Hitler was issued in Prague on 15 March 1939. The postmark records that Hitler was now *Kancléře* (Chancellor) of Czechoslovakia. On 15 March (the Ides of March) the new Chancellor – or rather, invader – took a special train from Berlin to the Czech border. From there he drove into Prague at the head of a convoy of ten motor vehicles. He was soon followed into the country by his troops. The bloodless conquest provoked a more outraged reaction than Hitler had anticipated. Even Chamberlain, in a speech he made in Birmingham, hinted that Great Britain was capable of rising to an aggressive challenge.

German: Pub. O. Struck, Berlin. 15 March 1939. Value C.

197

198

199

198. Adolf Hitler

This idealised portrait of Hitler was painted by Bruno Jacobs, an artist whose Jewish-sounding name was ironic at a time when Hitler's anti-Semitic policies were shocking the civilised world. The picture exemplifies Hitler's conservative, even reactionary, taste in art and his personal interpretation of how a leader should look: resolute, far-seeing eyes, but with gently shaped lips and a healthy hue to the cheeks. This romantic view of the wholesome, robust German type coloured all Hitler's selections for the opening exhibition in the House of German Art (q.v.) in July 1937. At the same time, Hitler's subjective choice of 'decadent' art – examples of some of Germany's finest expressionist paintings, 'Yiddish', negro and Marxist works – were also being exhibited in Munich. The 'degenerate' art exhibition drew bigger crowds than the banal, Hitler-approved exhibits.
German: Pub. Hoffmann. No. 445. Value C.
Colour illustration on page 76.

199, 200. Adolf Hitler

Hitler's uniform, including the Sam Browne belt, bears an extraordinary similarity to the British officer's service dress. While Hitler's entourage sported expensive plumage, he himself would often dress very simply. The cancellation on the reverse commemorates the Führer's visit to Vienna and has a written message: 'Dear Zenzl, I send you this card for your collection. Yours sincerely, Helen. Heil Hitler.'
German: Pub. Keystone, Berlin. No. 168. March 1938. Value C.

200

201   202   203

201. Chancellor Adolf Hitler

The Führer is wearing lederhosen, the leather shorts popular in Bavaria and Austria. He also has a black shirt, a uniform he styled upon Mussolini's Fascists and which was adopted by the SS, in contrast to the brown shirts of the SA. The reverse carries an adhesive stamp showing Hitler's head and shoulders and is cancelled *Geburtstag des Führers 20 April 1938*. The Führer's birthday. He was 49. German: Pub. Hoffmann. April 1938. Value C.

202. Julius Streicher

Streicher was one of the most important men in Hitler's immediate circle, particularly in the early years. He was obsessively anti-Semitic and propagated a violent anti-Jewish campaign through his weekly newspaper, *Der Stürmer*, which had been founded in 1922. On 1 April 1933, just days after Hitler gained effective control over Germany and dissolved the Weimar Republic, Streicher, through *Der Stürmer*, proclaimed a nationwide boycott of Jewish shops. Gangs of SA thugs enforced what was essentially an official edict.
German: Pub. Hoffmann. No. 680. *Circa* 1937. Value D.

203. R. Hess, The Führer's Deputy

Rudolf Hess, like Hitler, served in the 16th Bavarian Reserve Regiment during the First World War and joined the National Socialist party at the end of 1919. He, Rosenberg and Hitler, formed the nucleus of the NSDAP, and his contributions ranged from formidable pugilistics in the beer hall days, to typing *Mein Kampf* while he and Hitler were in prison at Landsberg, following the failure of the 1923 Munich putsch. He became the Führer's Deputy and

major fund raiser, tapping the fortunes of Fritz Thyssen, the steel magnate, and Carl Bechstein, the piano maker. To his Leader's surprise, he flew to Scotland on 10 May 1941, hoping to negotiate a peace with Britain. He was jailed for the duration of the war and then given life imprisonment at the Nuremberg Trials. In 1979 it was suggested that the 'Hess' in the Spandau prison in Berlin was an imposter.
German: Pub. Hoffmann. No. 306. *Circa* 1937. Value D.

204. Oberst von Epp

Franz Ritter von Epp first came to Hitler's attention in 1919, when his Free Corps unit helped overthrow Munich's soviet government. In March 1933 he was appointed State Commissar of Bavaria after Hitler's narrow majority in the Reichstag elections. Epp was, however, a deeply religious man, and he openly criticised the SS for flouting the law, which he considered to be the foundation of the State. He it was who advised Hitler to court-martial, rather than execute, Röhm, when the latter was accused of plotting a putsch aimed at using his SA to challenge the army. Hitler vacillated, but breaking his promise to von Epp eventually sent Eicke to give Röhm the chance to commit suicide. Eicke actually shot Röhm. von Epp, who was made an honorary SA *Obergruppenführer*, often appeared close to the Führer in photographs – notably during Chamberlain's historic visit to Munich in September 1938. He was also cultivated by the ambitious Himmler.

This early postcard was posted in Munich on 18 September 1921 and shows Epp as a colonel, proudly displaying his *Pour le Mérite* award.
German: Value C.

204   205

205. Captain Ernst Röhm

Röhm was an ex-First World War Company Commander, whose cheek had been scarred and whose nose had been modified in active service, with whom Hitler felt a strong soldier's kinship. He became Commander of the SA in 1920 and was defended by Hitler when attacked by the socialist press for his homosexual practices.

'As long as he remains discreet about things', Hitler confided to his photographer, Hoffmann, 'his private life is of no interest to me'. Röhm's jovial manner masked his brutal nature, which infected the atmosphere of the early NSDAP meetings. He regarded the SA as his private army. Röhm made attempts to persuade Crown Prince Rupprecht of Bavaria to work with Hitler, while at the same time others of his aides were plotting to kidnap the prince. Both plans, however, lapsed in the concerted effort to organise the November Munich putsch. Röhm led his storm troopers to the district military headquarters, which he occupied. They were surrounded the next day by state police and army troops. It was to rescue Röhm that Hitler, Ludendorff, Goering and their followers marched towards the Feldherrnhalle, only to be mown down by a hail of bullets. Röhm had to surrender. While Hitler was in the Landsberg prison, Röhm formed his own organisation, the *Frontbann*, but Hitler, fearing opposition, forced him to resign from it. Röhm joined the Bolivian Army, but in January 1931 was persuaded to return to become Chief of Staff of the SA, now 60,000 strong. A new scandal broke over Röhm's homosexual practices, but again Hitler did not dismiss him as a result.

Röhm continued to regard the SA as a fighting force, in conflict with the army. On 1 January 1934 Hitler appointed him Minister without Portfolio, hoping to curb his martial ambitions, while restricting the role of the SA. Röhm refused to accept the restraint, and his relationship with Hitler deteriorated.

He ignored rumours of a plot by Goebbels, Goering and Himmler to remove him and on 7 June 1934 went on a month's leave to Bad Wiessel. Hitler was led to believe that Röhm was planning a putsch and, in a panic, personally drove to Bad Wiessel to arrest Röhm. Goering and the others had prepared a list of 'traitors' to be executed. The purge was bloody, but at the last moment Hitler pardoned Röhm, his old army comrade. Later he gave way under pressure from Goering and Himmler, and Röhm was given a revolver, so that he could commit suicide. This he did not do, and was finally shot by Brigadeführer Eicke on 1 July 1934.

German: Pub. Josef E. Huber. *Männer der Zeit* (men of the moment) No. 24. Photo by E. Smaus of Munich. Value D.

Emmy Sonnemann

206 **207** **208**

Dr. GÖBBELS
Ihr ladet uns ein: „Hinein in den Staat" und meint diese Provinz des Weltkapitals
Das könnte Euch so passen.

209

206. Reich Chief Forester Hermann Goering

Goering held an extraordinary range of jobs, or at least titles, at one time. While he was Chief Forester he was also head of the Luftwaffe, Minister-President of Prussia, a Cabinet Minister and overseer of Hitler's 'Four Year Economic Plan'. He loved to dress in fancy uniforms and to wear gold and jewels, and luxuriated in the opulent living to which his position gave him access. He was perhaps the best-liked personality of the Nazi hierarchy, apparently bluff and jovial. In reality he was brutally jealous of anyone that might cast a shadow upon his own importance, and his concern with self-gratification led to his loss of favour with Hitler as early as 1942.

German: Pub. Hoffmann. *Circa* 1937. Value D.

207. Commander Goering

Hermann Wilhelm Goering was a leading air ace of the First World War with twenty-two victories to his credit, and, after Baron von Richthofen's death, became one of the Red Baron's replacements as leader of the famous Richthofen Circus. He met Hitler in 1922 and joined the Nazi Party later that year, becoming Commander of the SA. He went on to be Hitler's right-hand man and, in September 1939, the Führer designated Goering as his successor. Goering's drive and panache built the Luftwaffe from small beginnings into a superbly efficient tactical air force. However, he was unable to fulfil his boast that the Luftwaffe, which he commanded as Field Marshal, would prevent enemy planes reaching German soil and he fell from favour. In the picture Goering is wearing at his throat, the insignia of *Pour le Mérite*, the coveted 'Blue Max' of Imperial Germany.

German: Pub. Hoffmann. No. 140. Value D.

208. Emmy Sonnemann

On 10 April 1935, Reich Marshal Hermann Goering married for the second time (his first wife, Karin, having died of tuberculosis in 1931). His bride was a blonde, ideal Aryan-type actress, called Emmy Sonnemann. The wedding in the Evangelical Cathedral, Berlin, was a splendid affair, the gifts worthy of a royal wedding, the guests led by the Führer, the ceremony performed by a bishop and a commentary of it relayed on the radio.

The new Frau Goering had as her luxurious home, Karinhall, the villa that Hermann had built on the site of a hunting lodge near Berlin, in memory of his first wife. Goering also refurbished a palace in the Potsdamerplatz district of Berlin (former residence of the Prussian Minister of Commerce) and built a house on the Obersalzberg, near Hitler's Berghof. On Tuesday 27 February 1945 Goebbels comments in his diary, 'The Führer is glad that Goering's wife has now moved to the Obersalzberg because she was a bad influence on him [Goering]'.

It is hard to imagine how anyone can have had any adverse effect on the arrogant, corrupt, brutal, monstrous, drug addict into which the brave First World War ace degenerated.

The Goerings had a daughter, called Edda, born in 1938.

German: Pub. Ross, Berlin. Photo by Binder. Value C.

209. Dr Goebbels

Goebbels is in splendid declamatory form in this 1926 political speech in Berlin. 'You have invited us here,' he announces, 'into the State, and this Province is worthy of being the Capital of the world. You deserve that it should be so.'

Josef Goebbels had joined the Nazi Party in 1925, after he had flirted with communism and others of the myriad political groups which sprang up after the First World War. When he threw in his lot with the NSDAP, he was strongly influenced by Gregor Strasser, party organiser for Goebbels' area – north Germany. Like Goebbels, Strasser had left-wing leanings, and at first, Goebbels felt torn between the Hitler and Strasser rival camps within the party. At one stage he even called for Hitler's expulsion from the party. But in April 1926 Hitler invited the faltering Marxist to Munich, giving him the full treatment of his irresistible charm. Goebbels succumbed, and fell ecstatically in love with Hitler, whom he pronounced a genius.

Hitler was now the supreme, indisputable head of the party, with the power to appoint his own choice of *Gauleiters* (local leaders). He rewarded the convert Goebbels (whose potential value to the party he had obviously spotted even at this early stage) by making him Gauleiter of Berlin. This was an appointment he was to take up in November 1926 and to hold for the rest of his life. It was an important post, and a big task: to take the strife-ridden capital and establish firm party control of it. He did it superbly, and ruthlessly, with a series of dramatic, often violent demonstrations. His first great propaganda coup in 1930 was the stage managing of the funeral of Horst Wessel, the insignificant Brownshirt, whose one claim to fame was that he wrote the words to one of the Nazi Party's most popular rallying songs, 'Die Fahne Hoch' (Raise the Banner!). Wessel was shot by the communist lover of the prostitute with whom he was living. Goebbels transformed the murder into a martyr's death. The funeral was an extravaganza which, predictably, provoked the communists.

Next came the burning of the Reichstag by Dutchman Van der Lubbe in February 1933. Goebbels and Goering blamed it on the communists who in turn blamed the Nazis. van der Lubbe was probably acting alone but Hitler had the party leaders arrested, and their HQ (the Liebknechthaus) confiscated.

In March 1933, Goebbels was promoted to the post for which, with his undoubted intelligence and cultural pretensions, he was ideally suited – Minister for Public Enlightenment and Propaganda.

His first controversial propaganda exercise in Berlin after his appointment was an infamous act of barbarism – the burning of so-called 'un-German' books. The works of distinguished authors and scientists like Einstein, Freud, Gide, Thomas Mann, Proust, Zola and H. G. Wells, were joined by the book *All Quiet on the Western Front*, which Hitler particularly loathed because of its anti-war message. (Its author, Erich Maria Remarque, was forced to leave Germany.) Goebbels organised students with lighted torches to march down Unter den Linden to the University of Berlin. There the SA helped them make a symbolic bonfire of the 'undesirable' literature.

In September 1933 Goebbels had another important-sounding post – President of the Reich Chamber of Culture – with the responsibility of virtually censoring all forms of the news media and the world of entertainment.

In November 1938, Berlin witnessed another of Goebbels' violent demonstrations, which was to outrage not only the outside world, but also other Nazi leaders. It was the *Kristallnacht* – the smashing of Jewish shop windows all over Berlin.

Goebbels remained in the Ministry of Propaganda during the Second World War. He continued to operate from Berlin and it was there he died, still loyal to the man who had inspired him in 1926.

In this photograph, Goebbels is flanked by the Berlin police on his right and the SS on his left. The SS soldier on his immediate left looks remarkably like Himmler (who had not always sported a moustache).

German: Pub. and photographer Hoffmann. Value D.

Familie Dr. Goebbels

210   211   212

210. Reichsminister Dr Goebbels

Josef Goebbels was born in Rheydt, in the Rhineland, of a devout catholic, lower-middle-class family. His mother was of Dutch descent and an habitual rumour was that Goebbels had some Javanese blood. If true this could explain his dark eyes and hair, which, with his small stature (just over 1.5 m) (5 ft) and club foot (which resulted from childhood polio), made him the antithesis of the ideal Aryan – tall and blonde.

His high cheek bones and piercing eyes, his well-shaped nose, and well-brushed hair, could make him appear quite handsome when viewed from the right angle. Seen in profile, however, his bulging and somewhat simian cranium made him eminently caricaturable – often as a monkey.

Goebbels dressed fastidiously – sometimes in direct contrast to the ill-fitting mackintoshes and Bavarian excesses of the Führer's early days. His voice, when not stridently used in an imitative echo of Hitler's own speech-making style, was deep and mellifluous. He used his position as President of the Reich Chamber of Culture to run a string of high-class mistresses.

Although the Goebbels' Berlin residence, near the Brandenburg Gate, was luxuriously furnished – as were all the top-ranking Nazis' houses – he led a comparatively frugal life style. This he deliberately did, to contrast his visible efforts to live and eat economically in times of national hardship and deprivation, with the gross extravagances of the likes of Goering.

Goebbels was vain, highly susceptible to outrageous flattery, a compulsive and imaginative liar. He was a shallow personality, of vacillating moods and passions and,

like Hitler (who knew exactly how to coax the best out of him), a dreamer and a failed achiever in the arts. Goebbels' secret desire was to be a famous dramatist or novelist. His doctorate had been in literature, and he used all his language training in the field which he brilliantly made his own – propaganda.

In this photograph, he wears Hitler's mark of esteem – the Gold Party Insignia – on his well-tailored jacket.
German: Pub. Albrecht & Meister. Photographer Sandau. Value D.

[96]

211. 'Familie Dr Goebbels'

Magda Goebbels came from a wealthy family. She was blonde, elegant, and shared her husband's adoration of Hitler. He welcomed her blatant admiration. (The day after Hitler was proclaimed Reich Chancellor on 30 January 1933, Frau Goebbels brought Hitler a bouquet of flowers in congratulation.)

In Berlin, after his appointment, Frau Goebbels often acted as hostess at intimate tea parties, where Hitler enjoyed the company of actresses. His platonic enjoyment was in contrast to Goebbels' all too physical delight in their company. Magda finally revolted when he became infatuated with a Czech film star called Lida Baarova. She insisted on Goebbels moving out of the family household. To take her mind off her marital problems, Frau Goebbels joined Albert Speer and a party of friends on a tour of Sicily and southern Italy in March 1939. The plot thickened when Goebbels' young secretary, Karl Hanke, who also accompanied the group, fell in love with Magda. Probably 'on the rebound', she decided she wanted to marry Hanke! Goebbels also wanted to marry Baarova. Hitler, however, who had been best man at their wedding in 1931, firmly put his foot down. Despite the perversions he seemed able to tolerate in Röhm and other homosexuals, he absolutely refused to condone marital infidelity among his entourage. It offended his idealised image of the healthy German family unit, of whom the anchor was a good wife and mother. An artificial reconciliation was arranged, celebrated by happy pictures at Obersalzberg.

Magda had previously been married to Quandt, by whom she had a son, Harald. By Goebbels she had six children, five girls and a boy. On Sunday, 22 April 1945 they joined their parents to share the last bizarre days of Hitler's life in the Berlin Bunker. The three eldest, pictured here with their parents, were Helga, Hilde and Helmut. The youngest three were Holde, Heddi and Heidi. Hitler, whom all the children called 'Uncle Adi', was fond of them, as he was of most children.

Their parents' relationship had not been warm since their enforced reconciliation, but Magda's obsession with Hitler caused her to agree with Josef's decision that when Hitler died, so should their entire family. Magda made a last, desperate plea to her beloved Führer not to take his own life, which he spurned. Accounts of the Goebbels' final hours vary, but it is most probable that on 1 May 1945, Magda Goebbels gave her children chocolates laced with a lethal dose of either poison or a soporific drug. Later she took a cyanide capsule. Her husband then shot her, took his own capsule, and shot himself. Magda Goebbels was wearing Adolf Hitler's own Gold Party Badge, which he gave her the day before his own suicide.
German: Pub. and photographer. Hoffman. Value C.

212. Himmler with Führer Group

The caption on the reverse of this card is *Der Führer mit seinem Getreuen in Bad Elster am 22. Juni 1930*. (The Führer with his faithful in Bad Elster on 22 June 1930.) The 'faithful' include von Epp and Goering to Hitler's left, with Goebbels just behind him and Himmler on his extreme right (with glasses). As the entourage is visiting Bad Elster, others of the group are probably local party members.

Himmler was born in Munich in 1900. He was named after Prince Heinrich of Wittelsbach, whom Himmler's father tutored, and had an uneventful middle-class childhood. He was eager to join the army and managed at the age of seventeen to enlist in the 2nd Bavarian Infantry Regiment. When the war ended in November 1918 he was still an officer cadet and had never seen active service. After the war he joined the *Freikorps* and enrolled in Munich's Technical College as an agriculture student. He joined the NSDAP and by the time of the 1923 Munich putsch he had risen to the position of standard bearer of Röhm's *Reichskriegflagge*. When Röhm was imprisoned for his part in the abortive putsch, Himmler became political agent to Gregor Strasser, the leftist NSDAP member who also introduced Goebbels to the inner sanctum. It was at about this time that Himmler became obsessed with ancient German origins – history, religion, rites and lore. His agricultural training drew him to the peasantry, and concepts of strength through racial purity. He forsook his catholic religion and immersed himself in the mystical relationship between the blood and the soil of his native land. Himmler became an unbelievable paradox – a mild-mannered, totally unremarkable, non charismatic personality who through the medium of the SS, the *Schutzstaffel* (which literally means protective squad) developed into a monster of terrifying bestiality. The SS had been initiated by Hitler himself in 1925, to combat the dangerous power of Röhm's SA (*Sturmabteilung*, storm troopers). Röhm's SA wore brown shirts, the SS wore black, with the Runic 'S' flash of lightning, a solar symbol that was to become feared throughout Europe. On their black helmets they wore the Death's Head badge. When Himmler, failed chicken farmer, now married to a woman eight years his senior, became their *Reichsführer* in January 1929, he was to impose all his mystical quasi-religious eccentricities upon this elite band. He founded a secret association, called the *Ahnenebe* to carry out research into the ancient history of the German race. It was occult, with scientific and historical pretensions, and absorbed Himmler's time and energy. Another organisation he patronised, together with his fellow agriculturist, Darré (q.v.), was the RUSHA (*Rasse und Siedlungshauptamt* – Service of Race and Settlement). Despite these intellectual and theoretical pursuits, Himmler was indisputably responsible for the all too physical, horrific policy of exterminating the Jews and other racial 'undesirables'. The memorials to one of history's cruellest monsters are the concentration camps like Belsen, Buchenwald, Dachau, Malthausen and scores of others. Himmler ended his own life by taking a cyanide capsule on 22 May 1945, having been taken prisoner by the British.
German: Pub. and photographer Kohler-Tietze, Bad Elster. 1930. Value D.

Admiral N. von HORTHY.
Reichsverweser von Ungarn.

213   214   215

213. Reichsminister Dr Todt

Born in 1891, Todt was the architect and mastermind of the autobahn system of motorways, started after Hitler came to power in 1933. He had joined the Nazi Party in 1922 and soon gained Hitler's confidence and respect. A quiet, unassuming, sensitive personality, he kept himself withdrawn from the infighting and intrigue of the close circle that surrounded Hitler. The Führer nevertheless gave him more and more responsibility and authority. After the autobahn project, the building of the great defensive systems of the West Wall and the Atlantic Wall were entrusted to what became known as 'The Todt Organisation'. In 1940 he held the joint positions of Minister of Armaments and Munitions, and supreme head of all construction and defensive programmes. After his accidental death in a plane crash on 8 April 1942, Todt was quickly replaced by Albert Speer, who at one time had planned to accompany Dr Todt on his fatal flight. The question of sabotage of the aeroplane was never satisfactorily answered. Certainly there was friction between Todt and Goering, and because Todt wore the uniform of an air force Brigadier-General he was technically subordinate to Reich Marshal Goering.

German: Pub. Röhr, Magdeburg. No. 3530 Value D.

214. SS Major Skorzeny

Hitler's favourite SS soldier, and known as 'the most dangerous man in Europe', Otto Skorzeny was a flamboyant dare-devil, who pulled off some of the most spectacular coups of the war. Born in 1908 in Vienna, he was an early member of the Nazi Party and the SS. On 12 September 1943 he led a detachment of the SD (*Sicherheitsdienst*) to snatch Mussolini from captivity by the Badoglio government in a small hotel in the Abruzzi mountains. In October 1944 he boldly kidnapped the son of the Hungarian leader, Horthy, part of the punishment devised by Hitler when Horthy tried to prevent the deportation of Hungarian Jews. In December 1944, the unconventional Skorzeny was chosen to organise 'Operation Grief' – code name of the plan to infiltrate the Allied lines by Germans dressed as American soldiers. Although many of Skorzeny's bogus GIs were caught and shot, their leader was acquitted as a war criminal in 1947, moved to Spain and died, a successful businessman, in 1975.

German: Pub. Hoffmann. No. R174. *Circa* 1943. Value D.

216

215. Admiral N. von Horthy

Although the postcard is captioned 'N' (for Nicholas) Horthy, the Hungarian Admiral is usually referred to by the Hungarian form of his Christian name – Miklós. The card was published in August 1938 to celebrate the visit to Germany of the *Reichsverweser* (administrator) and bears three special commemorative postmarks: Kiel, on 22 August, Berlin on 25 August, and Nürnberg on 27 August. Horthy became Regent of Hungary in 1920 and his régime was supported by the Nazi government during the 1930s. Relations between the two leaders deteriorated when the war began to go badly for Germany and their mutual distrust grew apace. In March 1944 Hitler sent German troops into Hungary. That summer Horthy attempted to prevent the deportation of Hungarian Jews and in October he negotiated an armistice with the Soviet Union. As a result, Hitler sent Otto Skorzeny into Hungary to discipline Horthy. This he did by kidnapping Horthy's son Miki by rolling him up in a carpet à la 'Caesar and Cleopatra', by capturing the Admiral's Citadel and deporting him to Austria. There Horthy remained until liberated by the Americans in May 1945.

German: Pub. Otto Hoppé. Picture No. 81. Value C.

216. General Admiral Dr h.c. Raeder (h.c. = *honoris causa*, indicative that doctor was an honorary title)

Erich Raeder was born in Hamburg–Wandsbek in 1876. He joined the navy in 1894 as an officer cadet and passed out as 'best student of the year'. He had a variety of appointments before the First World War, including a spell on the Royal Yacht, *Hohenzollern* which, however, he found boring. During the war he served on SMS *Seydlitz*, taking part in the Battle of Jutland. He was Naval Representative to the Armistice Commission in 1918 and, ironically, as Commander-in-Chief of the Navy, accompanied Hitler on his triumphant visit to Compiègne to accept France's surrender in 1940.

In the inter-war years he was Commander-in-Chief of Sea Forces, North Sea, then commanding Admiral in Kiel, and, finally, Chief of the German Navy. In January 1943, he was succeeded by Dönitz and after his somewhat forced resignation, was given the title, *Admiral Inspekteur der Kriegs marine*, a position which Speer scathingly described as entitling him 'solely to the privilege of a State funeral'.

The Admiral, a traditional, deeply religious officer of the old school, had frequent differences of opinion with Hitler and his Nazi cronies like Goering and Speer. Hitler had totally misled Raeder about the planned date for the outbreak of war. When it came in 1939, the Admiral felt his navy was totally inadequate to take on Britain's mighty fleet. The most serious altercations were over the plans for Operation 'Sea Lion' (the invasion of England), Operation 'Barbarossa', the Baltic naval campaign and Hitler's obsession with scrapping the surface fleet in favour of submarines. It was the latter which was the final straw for Raeder. Hitler had tried to keep him sweet, presenting him with Willem van der Velde's painting 'A Naval Battle' for his birthday, and awarding him the coveted Gold Party Badge for outstanding services to the German nation.

When Raeder learned the whole truth about Nazi atrocities, he destroyed the badge (which he is shown wearing in this photograph).

Grand Admiral Raeder was sentenced to life imprisonment at the Nuremberg Trials, but was released from Spandau because of ill health in 1955. He died in 1960.

German: Pub. *Die Wehrmacht* (illustrated war-time magazine). Photographer Sage und Binz. Value D.

217   218   219

217. Der Oberbefehlshaber der Kriegsmarine, Gross Admiral Doenitz

Born in the Berlin suburb of Grunau in 1891, Karl Doenitz came from a non-military Prussian family. During the First World War he served on the cruiser 'Breslau' until 1916, when he transferred to submarines and commanded U-boats U-39, UC-25 and UC-68. When the latter was sunk off Sicily in October 1918, Doenitz was taken prisoner and spent some months in captivity. During the next fifteen years his career progressed steadily, with all his time spent in the surface navy. In July 1935 Doenitz returned from a successful flag-showing, Far-East cruise as Captain of the cruiser 'Emden' (the first large warship to be built by Germany after the First World War and which was named after the famous First World War cruiser put out of action by the 'Sydney' off the Falklands in 1914).

The Treaty of Versailles had perhaps imposed the cruellest terms of all on the German Navy. Hitler, whose main motivation was to renounce Versailles, encouraged the bogus private 'Development Bureau' company set up in Holland with the real purpose of keeping Germany abreast of modern underwater boat technology. This was achieved by appointing German experts to conduct inordinately long sea trials on the submarines legitimately built for foreign nations. When the Anglo-German Naval Agreement of June 1935 permitted more German submarines to be built (45 per cent of the British strength) Germany was ready with a number of modern, partly-constructed U-boats. Grand Admiral Raeder needed a bright, experienced commander for the new 'Weddigen' flotilla, as the submarine fleet was called (after the heroic First World War U-boat captain).

He appointed Doenitz, then a Kapitän, as Flag Officer for Submarines. Naval experts assess the appointment as almost accidental, but as one which Raeder was to consider a great success in retrospect.

Doenitz soon exerted a strong influence on the technical and tactical policy of the U-boat fleet, placing much emphasis on training and drill. He innovated the 'wolf-pack' concept, which was to wreak such havoc on Allied convoys during the Second World War.

When war was declared, Raeder decided to keep Doenitz in charge of submarines, of which he had fifty-seven, only thirty-nine of which were sea-worthy. In October 1938, after a series of daring submarine operations, Doenitz was promoted to Rear-Admiral and continued to be a popular leader, who took a personal interest in all his men.

When the USA entered the war after Pearl Harbour, Doenitz successfully deployed submarines in US waters (in 'Operation Drumbeat') against US merchant shipping.

He was elevated to the rank of *Gross* (Grand) Admiral and the appointment of Commander-in-Chief of the Navy, succeeding Raeder in January 1943. It was at this stage that he stood firm against Hitler's wish to scrap surface ships in favour of submarines. A Prussian of the old school, Doenitz was virtually apolitical, having been trained to obey orders instinctively. He saw the NSDAP as a force which had put Germany back on its feet after the First World War, and therefore remained loyal to Hitler, while never being cowed by him when his naval expertise was challenged.

It is therefore ironic that it was Doenitz whom Hitler appointed as his successor in the last desperate days in the Berlin Bunker. On Hitler's death on 30 April 1945,

Bormann radioed Doenitz with the news. Despite misgivings, Doenitz eventually decided it was his duty to accept the position. On 23 May he and his entire staff were arrested by the British. Tried as a war criminal in the Nuremberg Trials, Doenitz served ten years' imprisonment in Spandau prison.

In this photograph, Gross Admiral Doenitz, Commander-in-Chief of the Navy, wears the Knight's Cross with Oakleaves at his throat. On his left breast he wears the Second World War U-boat Badge (but not the special gold, diamond-encrusted version made for him by Schwerin of Berlin), the 1939 clasp, the Iron Cross and the First World War U-boat Badge.
German: Pub. Bauer, Berlin. *Circa* 1943. Value D.

218. Field-Marshal Fritz Erich von Manstein

von Manstein was regarded as one of the most astute military minds of the Wehrmacht. A professional soldier (joining the 3rd Guards Regiment in 1906 at the age of nineteen), he gained useful experience during the First World War, and graduated from the War Academy. He was promoted to Major in 1927, Lieutenant-Colonel in 1931, Colonel in 1933, Major-General in 1937, and in 1939 became Chief of Staff to the Commander-in-Chief East. In Poland he was von Rundstedt's Chief of Staff and his plans for a thrust through the Ardennes and sweep to the Channel for the invasion of France in 1940, which coincided with Hitler's own, were adopted.

His brilliant successes during the Phoney War and the Invasion of France led to von Manstein's promotion to General of Infantry in June 1940, and his transfer to the Russian Front.

On 3 September 1941 he gained command of the Eleventh Army, and after a bitter winter campaign succeeded in recapturing the Kerch Peninsula in January 1942, when he was appointed Colonel-General. In June, he captured Sevastopol and a delighted Hitler promoted him yet again – to Field-Marshal – on 1 July.

In November 1942, von Manstein took command of 'Army Group Don' to divert Russian attention from the hard-pressed defenders of Stalingrad. The ploy failed to relieve the plight of Paulus's beleagured Sixth Army and Hitler was reluctant to authorise von Manstein to help them break out. The result was disastrous. Eventual surrender was inevitable, and the survivors were massacred.

von Manstein was next involved in the abortive 'Operation Citadel', mounted on 4 July 1943 against Kursk. He openly blamed Hitler for many of the bad decisions taken in the campaign and his relationship with the Führer deteriorated.

At the great January 1944 gathering of senior officers at Rastenburg, von Manstein's sarcastic response to Hitler's exhortation to fight to the last man incurred the Führer's wrath. Nevertheless, he was nervous of committing himself wholeheartedly to von Stauffenberg's conspiracy to assassinate Hitler.

Respect for von Manstein's intelligence and ability was virtually unanimous – from his fellow officers (like Blumentritt), from Hitler (despite von Manstein's outspoken criticisms) and from allied generals and historians. Indeed Liddell Hart fought against Field-Marshal von Manstein's sentence of 18 years' imprisonment as a war criminal at the Nuremberg Trials. The sentence was reduced considerably and von Manstein eventually died in 1973 in freedom.
German: Pub. Hoffmann, Munich. No. 1584. Postally used 22.7.43. Value C.

219. General Field-Marshal Kesselring

Albert Kesselring's career has many parallels with von Manstein. Both were professional, pre-First World War soldiers (Kesselring joined the 2nd Bavarian Foot Artillery Regiment at the age of nineteen) who served during that war with distinction (in Kesselring's case in Lorraine, in Russia and in Lille). During the Second World War Kesselring and von Manstein were generally considered to be the most able and consistent German generals, respected by their peers and their opponents alike.

Kesselring transferred to the Luftwaffe in 1933, was befriended by Goering and quickly promoted. In 1939 he commanded Air Fleet 1 in Poland and in January 1940 took command of the Air Fleet 2.

In July he became the third Luftwaffe officer to be promoted to Field-Marshal, and in September directed operations against the RAF in The Battle of Britain, the prelude to the proposed invasion of Britain 'Operation Sea Lion'. He then switched his attention to the bombing of London and the fearful Blitz campaign.

In 1941 the 2nd Air Fleet was transferred to the Russian Front, where Kesselring was eager to attack Moscow. He was moved yet again, however, this time to Italy, where he was appointed Commander-in-Chief South. Kesselring's task was now to co-ordinate operations with Rommel, whose superior he technically was. But Rommel was often irritated by Kesselring's optimism, a quality which gave him his nickname of 'Smiling Albert'.

It was in combating the Allies' advance after the invasions in Italy that Kesselring gained universal respect for his defensive operations. Having almost defeated Mark Clark's army as it landed at Salerno, Kesselring made maximum use of Italy's natural barriers – rivers and mountain ranges. The defence of Monte Cassino, with the attendant emotional factor of the bombing of the historic Abbey by the Allies, equates in German military history to the British evacuation from Dunkirk. In March 1945 Kesselring took over from von Rundstedt as Commander-in-Chief West of an exhausted, ill-supplied German Army. Transferred in the dying days of the war to the position of Commander-in-Chief South, he eventually surrendered his army on 3 May 1945.

Kesselring was tried as a war criminal and sentenced to death in May 1947. Later that year, the death penalty was commuted to life imprisonment and the former Field-Marshal served in prison until 1952. He died in 1960, having spent the last years of his life as Chairman of the German Veterans' Organisation, the *Stahlhelm*.
German: Pub. Hoffmann. Munich. No. 1529. Value D.

220   221   222

220. Field-Marshal Rommel

The Desert Fox, Erwin Rommel, is the German general most British people commonly associate with the Second World War. He gained their respect as Commander of the Afrika Korps in the 1940–42 western Desert campaigns. Rommel served with distinction in the First World War, winning Imperial Germany's highest award for bravery, *Pour le Mérite*, which can be seen in the picture beneath his Knight's Cross. Between the wars Rommel had several appointments, including a period at the Wiener Neustadt Military Academy, where the inventor of the postcard, Dr Emanuel Hermann, had taught half a century earlier. Like Guderian and Patton, Rommel led from the front and was often out of touch with his headquarters staff. Oddly, exactly that situation arose at Army Group B when the Allies landed in Normandy on 6 June 1944. Rommel had spent seven months strengthening the coastal defences, but was away celebrating his wife's birthday the day the invasion began. He was implicated in the 20 July 1944 bomb plot and was forced to commit suicide on 1 October 1944. German: Pub. Hoffmann. No. 1520. *Circa* 1943. Value D.

221. General Field-Marshal Keitel

Field-Marshal Keitel was the 'Yes-man' through whom Hitler was able to control the Wehrmacht. In 1938 the War Ministry was headed by Field Marshal Blomberg, and he and other senior Nazi military leaders, such as Fritsch, were not supporters of the Führer's aggressive diplomacy. Hitler's opportunity to overcome their opposition came in January 1938, when Blomberg, a widower of six years, was married. His bride, a typist in the Field-Marshal's office, turned out to have been a prostitute. Hitler, horrified, used the scandal as an excuse to look for a replacement for Blomberg. The logical choice was Fritsch, but Goering produced evidence that he had committed homosexual acts and was therefore unsuitable. Hitler was thus rid of two unco-operative people and he further consolidated his position by taking the post of Commander-in-Chief for himself, with Keitel as his Chief of Staff. Hitler described Keitel as 'Loyal as a dog', while the Wehrmacht Command called him 'Hitler's lackey'.

When Hitler received the news of the capitulation of France with obvious glee, Keitel remarked, 'Mein Führer, you are the greatest military captain of all time'.

He had been with Hitler when Colonel Stauffenberg's assassination attempt failed, and hugged his Führer in a delirium of joy on finding him still alive after the explosion, thereby ensuring his own continued favour.

Keitel's faithfulness was rewarded (if that is still the word at this desperate hour) by being appointed Supreme Commander of the German Armed Forces in Hitler's Berlin Bunker on 23 April 1945. But while Hitler still lived, he transferred his allegiance to Himmler, whom he felt would assume the leadership on the Fuhrer's death.

Realising he had backed the wrong man, Keitel soon reported to Doenitz, but he it was who had the ignominy of signing the surrender to the Russians in Berlin on 8 May 1945. To Albert Speer's disgust, Keitel relished the lavish meal, complete with caviare and champagne, his victors offered after the ceremony.

Tried as a war criminal at Nuremberg, Keitel was given the death penalty, and was hanged on 16 October 1946.
German: Pub. Hoffmann. Munich. No. 1146. Value D.

223

224

222. Field-Marshal von Kleist

Paul Ludwig Ewald Baron von Kleist was a German Cavalry General of the old school, who was retired by the Nazis in 1938. He was not a party member, but was brought back to service in 1939. In Poland he commanded the XXII Panzer Corps and in France in 1940 his Panzer group included Guderian's XIX Corps, and, although the latter later criticised his Commander, Kleist gained formidable victories in both campaigns. He was appointed Field-Marshal on 1 February 1943. In Russia he again did well, although he was reprimanded by Hitler when Rostov had to be given up. When, in March 1944, Kleist recommended withdrawal behind the line of the Dniester river, the Führer relieved him of his command.

German: Pub. Hoffmann. Value C.

The following four powerful and striking portraits (the artist is not credited) were produced for propaganda purposes by the British in neutral Portugal. The quotations have been very carefully chosen to show a pronounced anti-Nazi ring from speeches by some of Hitler's most prestigious high-ranking officers.

223. Rear-Admiral Lützow

Statement by the Rear-Admiral on German radio in February 1942 to the effect that the German Navy was not strong enough at the outbreak of war and, in spite of efforts since, it still was not strong enough to gain mastery of the sea. Comment below, 'How right the Admiral was'.

Lützow's main claim to fame was in the pocket battleship which bore his name. Launched in 1931 as the 'Deutschland', with the claim that she could outrun any ship she could not outgun, Hitler rechristened her 'Lützow' in 1940. He feared the adverse propaganda effect should a ship called 'Deutschland' be lost. The 'Lützow' survived a variety of encounters, to be finally scuttled in May 1945.

British: No. 51–2394. Value B.

224. Field-Marshal von Leeb

'Whoever achieves great success in the field of politics must not consider himself as possessing any knowledge of military science simply by having read the works of Clausewitz or von Moltke – or because once in the past he served in the ranks with the position of corporal' – Leeb 1937. Hitler, a corporal in the First World War, assumed supreme command of the German Army on 19 December 1941.

Wilhelm Ritter von Leeb was born in Bavaria in 1876. After serving with the German Expeditionary Corps in China during the Boxer Rebellion, and through the First World War, he continued in the army during the inter-war period. Ironically, in 1923, as Commander of the Bavarian Artillery, he took an active part in crushing Hitler's Munich putsch. Despite this, Hitler recalled him from retirement in 1938 to command the army that moved into the Sudetenland. He was promoted to Field-Marshal in 1940 but acquitted himself badly (in Hitler's eyes) at Leningrad and resigned his command. Leeb was captured by the Americans in May 1945, was tried as a war criminal, and served three years in prison. He died in 1956.

British: No. 51–2378. Value B.

225

226

227

225. Field-Marshal von Rundstedt

'For a continental power desirous of destroying England to have any probability of achieving victory, he must necessarily ally himself with Russia or with the United States.' From a lecture by von Rundstedt on a staff course. von Rundstedt did not fit easily into the plebeian Nazi mould. He was born in 1895 of an aristocratic Prussian family with a strong military tradition. von Rundstedt continued the success pattern, attaining the position of Chief-of-Staff of Corps on the Western and Eastern Fronts in the First World War, and Supreme Commander, Western Europe in 1944. He was temporarily removed from his command on 6 July when he made known his views that Germany should sue for peace, but was reinstated in September. von Rundstedt finally retired from active duty in March 1945, but was taken prisoner on 1 May. Because of his failing health he was never tried as a war criminal and died in Hanover in 1953.
British: No. 51–2378 Value B.

226. Field-Marshal von Rundstedt

'The time factor always works against whichever continental power wages war against England. This happened in the past and is still true in the present.'
From a lecture by von Rundstedt on staff course.
British: No. 51–2394. Value B.

227. Field-Marshal von Runstedt

On 1 October 1920, Karl Rudolf Gerd von Rundstedt, having just left the old German Army, joined the Reichswehr as a Lieutenant-Colonel. By 1932 he was a full General. In 1936 he represented the Wehrmacht at the funeral of King George V in London and in 1938 commanded the Second Army, with the task of marching into Silesia if the Munich talks failed. He retired on 31 October 1938, but was recalled to lead Army Group South when war began in 1939. He was 64. His ideas were largely responsible for the German breakthrough in France in 1940, but he was defeated on the Ukranian Front in 1942. In the German preparations for the Allied Channel assault he clashed with Rommel, who believed that the enemy should be stopped on the beaches, and not inland as Rundstedt maintained. He was captured by the Americans and served three years in prison, partly in Britain, where he was extensively interviewed by Liddell Hart. He was probably Germany's oldest soldier, and certainly one of the most respected. Here he is photographed carrying his splendid Field-Marshal's baton. Goering's even more flamboyant, be-jewelled baton is exhibited at the West Point Academy's Museum.
German: Pub. Film Foto, Berlin. No. C2233. Posted 8.2. 43 Value D.

228   229   230

228. Colonel-General von Brauchitsch

It was part of Hitler's policy to keep the army independent of the Nazi Party. In this way he hoped to retain the continuing co-operation of the Senior Officer Corps of the Wehrmacht. In 1938, Brauchitsch was chosen as head of OKH and Commander-in-Chief of the Army, in preference to the openly pro-Nazi Reichenau. But Brauchitsch was unable to stand up to the Führer and wielded no influence with him. He was blamed for the failure to capture Moscow in 1941 and dismissed. When Hitler ordered the destruction of Paris, Walter von Brauchitsch is credited with saving the city. In this photograph he seems to have forgotten to pin on his medal ribbons.

German: Pub. Hoffmann. Value D.

229. Colonel-General Model

Walther Model is ranked by some military historians alongside von Manstein and Kesselring. He was the youngest, next to Rommel, to hold the rank of Field-Marshal. His rapid rise (he was Colonel in 1939) is sometimes attributed to his strong allegiance to the Nazi Party and to his good relationship with Hitler. But he became known to some as the 'Führer's Fireman', because of his success in rebuilding broken fronts – particularly following 'Operation Citadel', the Kursk–Orel offensive in the summer of 1943. His most dramatic, if to him small-scale operation, was his improvised defence at Arnhem, which was a major factor in the failure of 'Operation Market Garden' in September 1944. After the Allies crossed the Rhine in April 1945, he found his forces surrounded and, in a quiet wood near the Ruhr town of Duisberg, he shot himself.

German: Pub. Hoffmann. No. R82. *Circa* 1942. Value D.

230. Colonel-General Heinrici

Heinrici was a professional soldier, originally an infantryman, who commanded his forces without resorting to the brutality which many generals showed, both towards their own men and the enemy. For some time he served under Guderian at the beginning of 'Operation Barbarossa'. He then commanded XL Panzer Corps on the Dnieper Front, the German 4th Army, and, in March 1945, took over Army Group Vistula from Himmler, who had been trying his hand at being an army general.

German: Pub. Hoffmann. No. R208. Value C.

231   232   233

231. Colonel-General Guderian

Heinz Guderian served in the First World War, after which he specialised in the study and development of armoured warfare. In 1938 he published his book, *Achtung! Panzer*, in which he set out the principles of future tank combat, including tactics such as rapid movement, supported by air power, on a narrow front. Commanding a Panzer Group in 1940, he was the first to cross the Meuse (at Sedan) and the first to reach the Channel. In 1941 he argued with Hitler about the direction of the German effort in Russia and was dismissed. A tough, burly man who led from the front and was popular with his troops, Guderian was the Nazis' Patton. When the war ended, he surrendered to the Americans and no proceedings were taken against him. He wrote his memoirs, *Panzer Leader*, in 1952 and died aged 66 in 1954.

German: Pub. Hoffmann. Value D.

232. Colonel-General Heinz Guderian

This portrait is part of a series entitled *Der Führer und seine Generäle des Heeres* (The Führer and his army generals), published by arrangement with the Army High Command. There are at least twenty-five cards in the series.

Heinz Guderian was born in 1888 and his experience in the First World War made him an invaluable ally during Hitler's series of annexations in the late 1930s. He accompanied the Führer when he drove his tanks into Vienna. There he was met with a rapturous reception and his overcoat buttons were torn off for souvenirs. During the war, his popularity with Hitler fluctuated. When successful (as he was in Poland in 1939 and in France in 1940) he was in favour. When he disagreed with Hitler's policies (as he did in Russia in 1941) he was out of favour. Hitler turned to him again for help after the defeat of Stalingrad and promoted him to Inspector General of Armoured Troops. A further promotion to Chief of the General Staff was made after the assassination attempt on Hitler in July 1944, but in March 1945, he was virtually dismissed after again disagreeing with his Führer.

German: Pub, Ernst Steiniger. Value D.

233. Colonel-General Heinz Guderian

Heinz Guderian was Germany's greatest tank expert. By 1934, with the help of the War Minister, Blomberg, he had succeeded in persuading Hitler to form a tank battalion at Ohrdruf. In 1938 he was appointed General of Armoured Troops and gained tactical experience during the invasions of Austria and Czechoslovakia. By the time Poland was invaded, in September 1939, Guderian had seven Panzer divisions under his command.

234

235

236

This coloured portrait was painted in 1940, when Guderian was at the height of his popularity with Hitler and the German people, because of his brilliant performance in the invasion of France. He chose a path through the Ardennes, crossing the Meuse at Sedan and then thrusting with incredible speed with his Panzer corps through northern France to cut the Allies off in Belgium. The caption on the reverse translates 'Our armour: Colonel-General Guderian, creator and leader of our victorious tank forces'.
German: Pub. National League for Germans Abroad. Artist W. Willrich. Value D.

234. General of Tank Troops Hube
Hans-Valentin Hube led the 16th Panzer Division under Rundstedt in the invasion of Russia, later rising to command the 1st Panzer Army. In March 1944, his 22 divisions were trapped in a pocket north of Odessa between the Rivers Bug and Dniester. Hube and Army Group Commander von Manstein struggled with Hitler to obtain permission for the 1st Army to break out. Manstein was summoned to the Berghof where, after a furious argument, he obtained the Führer's consent to a compromise withdrawal. Much equipment was lost, but the army was saved and the line closed. Hitler rewarded von Manstein by dismissing him.
German: Pub. Hoffmann. No. R249. *Circa* 1943. Value C.

235. General Jordan
By the beginning of 1944 Soviet Russia had thirteen times more men under arms than Nazi Germany and her forces were pushing westwards from the Baltic to the Black Sea. Hitler's interference with his generals' conduct of their campaigns became increasingly irrational. He made his decisions intuitively, believing that he possessed some mystical military insight. Frequently his attitude was one of 'no withdrawal' and, in the vastness of the isolated Eastern Front, the lack of freedom for the German generals to organise strategic withdrawals resulted in the loss of whole armies. Some commanders overcame their fear of the Führer and acted upon their own military appreciations of the situation. Perhaps General Hans Jordan did that. He was dismissed from the command of the 9th Army for 'irresolute leadership' during the Russian spring offensive in 1944.
German: Pub. Hoffmann. No. R250. *Circa* 1943. Value C

236. Lieutenant Benzin
Benzin was a 'full' lieutenant, who in the British Army would wear two pips in contrast to the second lieutenant's one. The reason for his appearance on a postcard may have been his winning of the Knight's Cross with oak leaves, which can be seen at his throat. Over his left breast there is just visible a metal badge with outstretched oak leaves. Such emblems were awarded to those who took part in specific actions and raids.

Hoffmann probably photographed all those who won the Knight's Cross, certainly over 100 portraits are recorded.
German: Pub. Hoffmann. Value C.

237   238   239

237. Obersturmbannführer Frey

The badge of rank of this SS Lieutenant-Colonel is on his left-hand collar. He is a *Ritterkreuzträger* – a Knight's Cross holder, with the further distinction of oak leaves. The Knight's Cross was a class of the Iron Cross that was worn at the throat, as opposed to on the left breast, as were the first two grades of the award – the Iron Cross Second Class and the Iron Cross First Class.

Portraits of significant medal holders were probably taken at the time when Hitler up-graded the Iron Cross to the status of an Order, in 1939. The prefix R before Hoffmann's number could well refer to Ritterkreuzträger.
German: Pub. Hoffmann. No. R229. Value C

238. Kurt Student

As Guderian was Germany's 'tank man', so Student was their 'airborne man' *par excellence*. He commanded the German airborne forces throughout the war, forming separate parachute divisions. In 1939, on being promoted Major-General, Student created the first secret battalions of paratroopers. He was wounded in the fighting to take Rotterdam and was out of action until he planned the airborne operation in Crete in May 1941, a campaign that was extremely costly in German casualties. Student was bitterly frustrated when Hitler cancelled his proposed invasion of Malta, but he was a calmly philosophical man and remained loyal to Hitler throughout the war. In 1944 Student was appointed GOC 1st Parachute Army and, with Model, organized the defence of Arnhem. In December 1944 the Ardennes attack floundered and he was again disappointed when his proposed thrust to Antwerp was put off. In April 1945, Keitel and Jodl sought to have Student

put in charge of the defence of Berlin, but the move came too late to be implemented. Caption on reverse translated reads: 'General of Airborne Forces Student'.
German: Pub. for the National League for Germans Abroad. Artist W. Willrich. 1941. Value D.

239. General Wolfram, Freiherr von Richthofen

Wolfram, Baron von Richthofen, bore a famous family name – that of his cousin, Manfred, better known as 'The Red Baron' in the First World War. The young Wolfram had served in his illustrious relative's squadron during the war. After a short post-war spell as an engineer, he rejoined the army in 1923 and then transferred to the Luftwaffe. His career was eventful and brilliant. By 1938 he was a Major-General, having commanded the German Condor Legion during the Spanish Civil War. An extrovert, ebullient personality, he gained a reputation as an expert in ground to air co-ordination and co-operation during the Second World War.

His VIII Air Corps seemed to be everywhere: Poland, the Low Countries, France, and Crete, where it spearheaded the invasion in May 1941. In Crete, Richthofen commanded about 500 aircraft. In 1941 VIII Air Corps was transferred to the Russian Front, where their fierce attacks and frequent sorties gained them distinction at Kalinen and Sevastopol.

In the summer of 1942, Richthofen was promoted to Colonel-General to command 4th Air Fleet. In October he was required to supply Paulus's beleaguered 6th Army in Stalingrad, although he favoured a breakout attempt. February 1943 saw a further promotion for the Baron – to Field-Marshal, the fourth Luftwaffe officer to be so

240 **241**

honoured. That summer he was transferred to the Mediterranean, where he made an error in judgement, thinking that the Allies would move from Tunisia to invade Sardinia (rather than Sicily, as actually occurred). von Richthofen, although he questioned the rightness of some of his orders (as at Stalingrad) remained ostensibly loyal to Hitler and Goering to the end.
German: Pub. Rob. Rohr, Magdeburg. No. 3508. Value D.

240. Colonel-General Ernst Udet

Oberleutenant Udet was second only to the Red Baron von Richthofen in his total of sixty-two victories as a fighter pilot in the First World War, and spent many years in America between the wars as a stunt flyer. Goering, Colonel-in-Chief of the Luftwaffe, gave the job of aircraft production to his old friend Udet in 1937. He is said to have had a major role in conceiving and developing the Stuka dive-bomber but became the scapegoat for the failure of the Luftwaffe to control the sky over Europe. He fell out of favour with Goering and committed suicide in November 1941. The Nazi propaganda machine announced that he had died testing a new plane.
German: Pub. Hoffmann. Value D.

241. Oberst Mölders

Werner Mölders was one of the most popular and attractive Luftwaffe officers. Before the war he was Germany's youngest wing commander and a household name, gaining much experience with the Condor Legion in the Spanish Civil War.

At the outbreak of the Second World War, his career progressed apace with his achievements as one of the Luftwaffe's foremost aces. He was promoted to General (the first fighter pilot to gain this rank) after his hundredth kill. Mölders' air support had been a significant factor in Guderian's initial successes in the Russian campaign.

There his squadron, JG51, was the first fighter unit to attain the astonishing claim of 1,000 combat kills. Molders' succession of Messerschmitt Bf 109s were painted with his scores. On 14 May 1940 his Bf 109E–3 showed his tenth victory, an RAF Hurricane, brought down over Sedan. The Bf 109F–1 he flew during the Battle of Britain showed 55 victories (16 French and 39 RAF). He was awarded the Oak Leaves to his Knight's Cross on attaining his 40th. During the Russian campaign of autumn 1941, his Bf 109F recorded his 101 kills of the Second World War. These were in addition to the 14 he scored during the Spanish Civil War.

Mölders was posted from JG51 to become Inspector of Fighters, but he was killed in an air crash in November 1941.
German: Pub. Hoffmann. Munich. No. 1511b. Value C.

EL GENERALISIMO FRANCO
· por Jalón Angel·

GENE°M FANG
M. HSP. GIOR.

MOLA
por Jalón Angel

242   **243**   **244**

242. El Generalisimo Franco

Francisco Franco Bahamonde was born in 1892 in Galicia. He entered the Toledo Military Academy in 1907 and by 1920 was second in command of the Spanish Foreign Legion. He then became director of the General Military Academy at Saragossa. On 17 July 1936, Franco sparked off an army uprising in Spanish Morocco. He then returned to the mainland, where revolts had also broken out, and four days later the whole country was embroiled in a Civil War that was to last 2 years, 254 days and cost approximately 1 million lives.

Despite the help that Franco had received from his fellow Fascists, Hitler and Mussolini, he maintained a theoretical neutrality during the Second World War. His strong anti-communist stand, however, caused Franco to send a division of volunteers to fight with Germany in the Ukraine in June 1941. This, and Franco's occasional meetings with Hitler and Mussolini, caused the Allies to distrust Spain's supposed neutrality and Franco's peace-mongering in July 1943 after the fall of Italy.

After the Second World War, Franco's oppressive dictatorship was declared 'unfit to associate with the United Nations'. Gradually, the tight Falangist stranglehold was loosened, culminating in Franco's declaration in 1954 that the Infante, Don Juan Carlos, should be groomed as his heir, with the eventual restoration of the monarchy. Juan Carlos did, indeed, succeed to the Spanish throne on Franco's death in November 1975.

Spanish: Photographer Jalón Angel, Zaragoza. Pub. 'Arte', Bilbao. Series *Forjadores de Imperio* (The forgers of the State). Popular edition. Value C.

243. Generalisimo Franco

On 1 October 1936, General Francisco Franco assumed leadership of nationalist Spain (representing the Fascist uprising) in its fight against the leftist, Republican Party. In April 1937, the nationalist factions fused under the title *Falange Española Traditionalista*, with Franco as its *caudillo* (leader). He also assumed the title of *Generalisimo* (supreme commander) in 1939. Like his Fascist friend, Hitler, Franco quickly recognised the power of radio as a means of disseminating propaganda. The National Radio Station was in Burgos, which had been the nationalists' stronghold since before the Civil War. The reverse of this postcard bears an interesting message:

> '*Radio Nacional De España*
> 238′5 m(1.258 k.c/s.)–28′93 m(10.370 k.c/s.) English Broadcast for Europe: 21′15–12′30 G.M.T. Broadcast for USA & Canada: 2–3 G.M.T. We have pleasure in informing you that a book of Descriptive Talks (illustrated) by Florence Farmborough (Florence "Fairplay" of Radio Naçional), has just been published by Messrs. Sheed and Ward. 31, Paternoster Row, London. E.C.4, under the title of "Life and People in National Spain", at 2/6d. per copy. All profits on the sales will be devoted to the relief of the suffering children in Spain, irrespective of political antecedents.
> Department of Radio National. BURGOS (SPAIN).'

'Florence Fairplay' seems to have been the Falangist equivalent of the Nazi 'Axis Sally', 'Ann of Arnhem' and 'Lord Haw-Haw'.

Spanish: *Circa* 1939. Value C.

QUEIPO DE LLANO
por Jalón Angel

245

246

244. General Emilio Mola

In July 1936 a simultaneous revolt broke out in twelve Spanish military garrisons against the leftist coalition government of Manuel Azaña. General Mola concentrated the northern uprisings of Burgos, Saragossa and Huesca, making Burgos (which had for three years been the nationalist headquarters) his base. In July and August, Mola led 15,000 regular soldiers southwards as part of the concerted attack on Madrid. In October, Mola was coverging on Madrid, with four rebel columns. His announcement that he had a 'fifth column' in the city gave rise to the use of the term as a subversive force working against the establishment from within. General Mola died in an air crash on 3 June 1937.

Spanish: (Photographer Jalón Angel, Zaragoza. Pub. 'Arte', Bilbao). Series *Forjadores de Imperio* (The forgers of the State). Popular edition. Value C.

245. General Gonzalo Queipo de Llano

General de Llano commanded the military garrison in Seville in July 1936. He was one of the first military leaders to support the revolt againt Spain's second, abortive republic under the Marxist, Manuel Azaña and his ineffective Prime Minister, Santiago Casares Quiroga. Under their undisciplined and short-lived régime, Fascism thrived, as a protest against extreme socialist and republican violence. In November 1936, Franco's tenuous government was recognised by both Germany and Italy. In February 1937, Mussolini sent Italian troops to help his fellow Fascists. They joined de Llano's forces and succeeded in capturing Malaga, but were unable to cut the Madrid–Valencia road and thus speed the end of the siege of Madrid. In this postcard, de Llano uses the new propaganda medium of the radio, with a most splendid microphone.

Spanish: Photographer Jalón Angel Zaragoza. Pub. 'Arte', Bilbao. Series *Forjadores de Imperio* (The forgers of the State). Popular edition. Value C.

246. Il Duce

The Italian Fascist Party, the PNF, was founded in 1919 when Benito Mussolini, the man who was to lead the party to its greatest achievements and excesses, was still flirting with socialism. Seeing the emerging force as a tool for his ambition, Mussolini threw in his lot with the Fascists during the period of industrial unrest in 1920. His rise through the party was little short of meteoric, and in October 1922 King Victor Emmanuel III asked Mussolini to form a government. He was granted extraordinary powers to deal with the widespread anarchy and gradually he adopted the power and behaviour patterns of a dictator. In 1925 a law was passed granting him 'greater power of parliamentary initiative' and limiting the king's effectiveness. Mussolini was surrounded by weak, incompetent subordinates in comparison with whom he appeared strong, decisive and intelligent. Hitler was shrewd enough to realise that, by playing on Mussolini's colossal vanity, he could make an ally of him for Germany. Mussolini at one time feared, however, that Hitler would despise the Italians as 'non-Aryans', and Italian scholars were set to work to prove that the Italians were of Nordic stock.

Italian: Pub. R. Questura di Bergamo. Artist F. Spoltora. March 1941. Value D.

247 **248**

247. The Duke of Aosta

In 1922, as Mussolini's Fascists began to gain power in Italy, the popular Emanuele Filiberto, Duke of Aosta and hero of the First World War, sympathised with the Fascists. As cousin of the king, he was proposed as a prospective Fascist Pretender to the Italian throne. His son Amadeo, pictured here, was also to earn his place in Italian history. When the Second World War broke out he was Governor General of Italian East Africa, Viceroy of Ethiopia and was appointed Commander-in-Chief of Italian forces in the area. His force was numerically strong, although it consisted largely of colonial troops trained and equipped for security only and he used its strength to force the British out of British Somaliland. The British then launched a campaign to reclaim East Africa, which converged in a huge pincer movement on Amba Alagi, where the Duke made an heroic last stand. His eventual surrender was to save further useless loss of life and the British accorded him 'The Honours of War' for his gallantry. He died in British captivity in Nairobi in 1942.
Italian: Pub. S.A. Grafitalia, Milan. Artist A. Porni. 1941. Value C.
Colour illustration on page 76.

248. Umberto di Savoia

Umberto was the son of Victor Emmanuel III of the House of Savoy, King of Italy. He commanded Italy's Army of the Alps, attacking France in 1940. The three-pronged invasion by thirty-two Italian divisions, on 21 June, was repulsed by six French divisions, the one bright spot in France's tarnished military prowess that year. It could not prevent France's capitulation, however, which officially took place on 25 June 1940. Umberto assumed the Regency in 1944, when the Allies entered Rome, and after the war he reigned for a brief thirty-five days from May 1946 (when his father abdicated in his favour) to June 1946, as Umberto II. The Italians then voted to abolish the monarchy, and the rule of the House of Savoy, which had begun in the eleventh century, came to an end. Caption (translated) reads: 'With unshakeable faith the heroic vision of past triumph, the unfailing destiny of Imperial Italy is again on the march'.
Italian: Artist F. Spoltora. 1941. Value C.

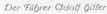
Der Führer Adolf Hitler

Der Duce Benito Mussolini

Hilde KÖNIGSBAUER
Gauführerin des B. d M.

249   **250**

249. The Führer, Adolf Hitler. The Duce, Benito Mussolini (Twin card)

After the successful negotiation of the 'Axis' agreement in September/October 1936 by Count Ciano on behalf of Mussolini, Hitler tried his utmost to persuade the Italian leader to come to Germany. Eventually Mussolini agreed, provided that he was not required to wear civilian clothes at dinner and that he could address a large crowd. Il Duce arrived in Munich on 25 September 1937 attired in a new Fascist uniform which had been designed for the occasion, to be met by Hitler in a plain Nazi Party uniform. These are probably the uniforms shown on this twin card. The card was issued in Berlin when the leaders went on to the capital two days later, each travelling on his own train. The event was superbly stage-managed, with almost 1 million spectators and over 50,000 SS to control the crowds. On 29 September Mussolini had his wish to address a crowd fulfilled and Hitler introduced him to a packed Olympic Stadium.

German: Pub. Alfred Oemler, Berlin. No. 1.113 and No. 1.114 (Mussolini).

Adhesive stamp on each card cancelled (translated) 'Mussolini–Hitler Rally, Berlin. 29 September 1937'. Value C.

250. 'Hilde Königsbauer. Gauführerin des B. d M.' (Regional Leader of the League of German Maidens)

Hitler saw the role of women in his ideal Folk State as important but limited. In his political and racial manifesto, *Mein Kampf*, when talking of the education of girls, he wrote, '. . . the chief emphasis must be laid on physical training, and only subsequently on the promotion of spiri-

tual and finally intellectual values. The goal of female education must invariably be the future mother.'

Although he was personally attracted to women who had aristocratic backgrounds, great beauty or outstanding talents (like Unity Mitford, Magda Goebbels, Leni Riefenstahl, or Hannah Reitsch), his official preference was for pure Aryan, healthy peasant types. He saw their purpose as providing good breeding stock. They had no place in the higher echelons of political decision making. 'I allow no man to stick his finger in my political pie', he told his friend and photographer, Hoffmann, 'And most certainly no woman!'

Hitler took a keen interest in the *Bund Deutscher Mädchen* and firmly rejected the original design of their uniform. He commented to Baldur von Schirach, Reich Youth Leader, when watching them march past, 'In old sacks like that the poor girls won't attract a single masculine glance. The Party is not here to bring up a race of old maids.' He ordered a fashionable Berlin couturier to design more feminine uniforms.

The Bund Deutscher Mädchen was run on similar lines to the Girl Guides, with heavy emphasis on outdoor physical activities. This regional leader may well have come from the Munich area as her photograph is taken by Hoffmann.

German: Pub. Hoffmann. No. 770. Value C.

251   252   253

251. 'Jungbäuerin' (Young country girl)

Jungbäuerin aus der Reichsschule für Leibesübungen des Reichsnährstands in Burg Neuhaus (Young country girl from the State school for physical training and nutrition in Burg Neuhaus).

The epitome of Aryan youth: blonde, healthy, tanned, unsophisticated. Quote on the reverse: *Es gibt nichts Kostbareres auf der Welt als die Keime edlen Blutes* (There is nothing so precious in the world as the seed of noble blood).

From breeding stock such as this, Hitler hoped to build his 1,000 year Reich. The quotation was by Walter Darré, Minister of Agriculture in 1933.

German: Pub. Racial Political Arm of the NSDAP. From the Calendar *Neues Volk* (New people) 1940. Value C.

252. 'R. Walther Darré Leiter der agrarpolitischen Abteilung NSDAP' (Leader of the Agrarian Policy Division of the NSDAP)

Dr Darré was a man who shared Hitler's idealist, somewhat mystical concept of the German nation and its stock. He had been born in Argentina in 1895 and served in the Artillery in the First World War. After the war he studied for his doctorate in Agricultural Engineering and wrote a book called *Das Bauerntum als Lebensquelle der nordischen Rasse* (The Peasantry as the Life Force of the Nordic Race). He joined the party in 1930 and then the SS, becoming in 1931 the first chief of RUSHA (*Rasse und Siedlungshauptamt* – Service of Race and Settlement). In June 1933, Hitler appointed him Minister of Agriculture in his first Cabinet and in 1934 *Reichsbauernführer* (national leader of the peasantry). In 1936 he clashed with Himmler and had to resign his position with RUSHA, which more and more controlled every aspect of the lives of the elitist SS. Among Darré's more revolutionary theories was the conviction that Christianity destroyed the purity of the Germanic philosophy.

Darré served a term of imprisonment as a war criminal and died in 1953. In this photograph he is wearing the badge of the SS.

German: Pub. Hoffmann. No. 130. *Circa* 1931. Value D.

253–256. Four portraits by W. Willrich

Wolf Willrich (q.v.), as a Nazi-approved artist, painted a complete picture gallery of all arms of the service. The series featured all ranks, from private to Field-Marshal; ordinary seaman to Admiral; airman to Air-Marshal, and included many Iron Cross and other award winners. Series titles included:

Fallschirmjäger (Parachutists)
Heer und Panzer (Army and tanks)
Luftwaffe (Air force)
Marine (Navy)

All were sold in aid of the VDA (*Volksbund für das Deutschtum im Ausland* — League for Expatriate Germans). Value C.

254   255   256

253. 'Unsere Panzerwaffe: Ein Kradschütze' (Our tank forces. A motorcyclist)

The motorcycle troop would be attached to the Panzer Division for reconnaissance purposes. During the Battle for the River Meuse in the invasion of France by the Germans in May 1940, the French attacked the German motorcycles at Wastia and achieved one of the few French successes of the campaign. It was, however, short lived, as the French tank crews became nervous at night and withdrew from the heights they had captured on 14 May. Card overprinted on reverse: 'German People's Fund for Fallen Comrades. German Youth September 1941.'

254. 'Unsere Panzerwaffe: Ein Panzer Pionier' (Our tank forces. A tank engineer)

By 1940 Germany had ten Panzer Divisions. Each division was a complicated mixture of self-contained battle groups, consisting of Rifle Regiments, Signals Battalions, Engineers and an Artillery Battalion to back up the main Panzer Regiment. After the invasion of Poland, several cavalry divisions were converted to Panzer Divisions.
(The name just visible on the picture is that of the subject) *Circa* 1940.
Colour illustration on page 76.

255. 'Unsere Luftlandetruppen: Hauptmann Delica' (Our airborne forces: Captain Delica)

Delica took part in the daring and brilliantly executed glider-borne coup to capture the supposedly impregnable Belgian fort at Eben Emael. He was an air force communications officer, whose task was to call in German air support should the paratroopers require assistance. In the event, his glider landed 500 m to the south of the main casemate and he was pinned down by heavy Belgian fire. At the time of the raid, on 11 May 1940, Delica's rank equated to Flight Lieutenant and he was second in command of 'Assault Force Granite' under Lieutenant Witzig.

The postcard is overprinted on the reverse: *Volks-deutsches Kamerad-schaftsopfer der Deutschen Jugend. February 1942* (The German Peoples' Fund for Fallen Comrades of the German Youth).

256. 'Unsere Luftlandetruppen: Luftlandepionier' (Our airborne forces: an airborne engineer)

Our un-named engineer looks like the explosives expert of the *Sturmabteilung* (storm group) in the plan which Hitler himself conceived for the taking of Eben Emael. General Student was given the task of planning the operation, which was to open the doorway to Dunkirk for the Germans. He used a highly effective new type of explosive, a *Hohlladung* (hollow charge), which proved capable of blowing the steel cupolas and reinforced concrete of the 'Maginot Line' type fort. The survivors of the raid (fifty-one out of seventy-seven) were all summoned to meet their exultant Führer. The officers were awarded the *Ritterkreuz* (Knight's Cross) and the men the Iron Cross.

[115]

257

258

259

260

261

262

257. Wedding photo

The year is 1939. Perhaps this ardent Nazi couple are getting married before the husband goes away to war. Hitler gave a copy of his book *Mein Kampf* as a wedding present to each party member. This certainly boosted the numbers printed.

German: Pub. and photographer A. Jemelka. Value B.

258. Wedding photo

The perfectly unlined face of this ideal Aryan bride, her bouquet of expensive carnations, her white dress and veil – all would indicate the optimism and confidence of the early days of the war.

German: Pub. and photographer Henk, Hollabrun. Value B.

263

264

259. Wedding photo

The handwritten message on the reverse of this happy wedding photograph is: *Zur Erinnerung; Wien ein Dezember 1940* (In remembrance of Vienna, 1 December 1940).

At the end of the second year of the war, economy begins to bite – no white wedding dress for the bride. The smart young NCO wears his peaked *Schirmmütze* (uniform cap) and *Waffenrock* (uniform tunic).

Austrian: Pub. and photographed by Maria Waclawowicz, Vienna. 1940. Value B.

260. Wedding photo

The young Luftwaffe *Obergefreiter* was married in Berlin on 17 November 1942. His rank can be recognised by the number of silver-grey wings on his yellow collar patches. *Flieger* (airman) carried one wing; *Gefreiter* (lance-corporal) had two; *Obergefreiter* (corporal) had three and *Hauptgefreiter* (a rank which has no immediate British counterpart, but which is somewhere between a corporal and a sergeant) four. It is interesting that even in the Second World War when National Socialism became the 'religion' of many soldiers, the standard belt plate still bore the First World War legend, *Gott Mit Uns*.

German: Pub. and photographer W. Junker. Value B.

261. Leave. April 1943

'Urlaub (leave) April 1943' is the hand-written caption to this happy photograph. The girl wears no wedding ring, but proudly and possessively holds her Obergefreiter (corporal), highlighting his rank chevrons. The reverse bears the rubber stamp with the name, address and telephone number of the Viennese photographer.

Austrian: Pub. and photographer Simonis of Vienna. 1943. Value B.

262. Silver wedding group

This harmonious, obviously devoted couple are extremely fortunate that they are still together to celebrate their silver wedding anniversary on 3 January 1945. The husband is an *Oberintendanturat* (a staff Lt. Col.) and a Knight's Cross of the Distinguished Service Cross with Swords, winner.

Austrian: Pub. and photographer Knozer, Vienna and Baden. Value B.

263. Family group

Just as in the First World War, there is little hope of the two young sons, so clean cut, so steadfast of gaze, returning whole from the war. In the dreadful man-against-man battles of attrition of the so-called 'Great War', roughly 3 million German and Austrian soldiers died. In the Second World War the death count was similar, although there were 3 million more wounded. The mother smiles confidently, but the father's wistful expression belies the anxiety of a survivor of the First World War.

Austrian: Pub. and photographer Wilhelm Donabauer, Vienna. Sepia. Value B.

264. Iron Cross Holder

This Panzer Grenadier Iron Cross holder wears his denims and tropical field cap (*Feldmütze*). Tanned and fit looking, he has probably seen service with Rommel in North Africa. Now he is in Naples, in the winter of 1943.

German: Pub. anon. 1943. Value B.

265   266   267

265. An old soldier

The wise eyes of this experienced soldier are those of a man in his forties, as many were in 1944/1945. He reminds one of Katz – the resourceful, skiving old soldier in *All Quiet on the Western Front*, Erich Maria Remarque's classic German story of the First World War. He tutors the innocent young soldiers in the art of survival, only to die himself. One wonders whether this soldier, immortalised on a Kodak postcard, survived the Second World War.
German: Value B.

266, 267. Two young soldiers

As our experienced Second World War soldier resembles Katz, so these young lads have the earnest, dedicated eyes of the German students who marched, singing, to the 'Massacre of the Innocents' in the First Battle of Ypres in 1914. Many of those young students, who are epitomised by Paul Baumer, the hero of *All Quiet on the Western Front*, lie with 44,000 of their comrades in Langemarck cemetery near Ypres. In the Second World War German cemetery at La Cambe in Normandy, many seventeen-, eighteen- and nineteen-year-old soldiers are buried. In the final, desperate struggle to hold Berlin, Hitler encouraged fourteen-, fifteen-and sixteen-year-old boys from the Hitler Youth Movement to fight to the death. From the early 1930s Hitler and his propaganda machine had concentrated on capturing the minds and will of Germany's children. The scheme was master-minded by Goebbels, a Doctor of Philosophy, who knew the vulnerability and malleability of young minds.

266.

This young soldier is in the 137th Infantry Division, which was formed in October 1940. It saw heavy action on the Russian Front in August 1941 and was also in the Kursk offensive in the summer of 1943. His name is John Ruoli and the photograph was taken to celebrate his joining the army.
German: Pub. and photographer F. Hartl, Salzburg. Value B.

267.

This young cadet would certainly have been called up before the end of the war.
German: Pub. and photographer König, Altenburg. Value B.

268. Airman

This Luftwaffe *flieger* wears a lanyard. These were awarded for marksmanship. Each arm of the service had an appropriate plaque or shield attaching the lanyard to the right shoulder – Panzer marksmen wore a design which incorporated a tank, for instance. Additional marksmanship awards were denoted by adding an acorn or a miniature shell (for the Artillery) for each successive achievement. The lanyards were worn with parade and walking-out uniform, as well as reporting and guard uniform.
German: Pub. anon. Value B.

268   269   270

269. Soldier in cap

This anonymous soldier has no badges or insignia visible to indicate his regiment. He wears the 1943 general issue field cap (*die Einheitsfeldmütze*). Based on the Afrika Korps cap design, with a long peak, and made of field grey cloth, it became the most widely worn form of headgear in the German Army. Panzer troops wore black caps, and camouflage versions were also made. Above the two buttons which secure the movable sides is the national emblem (*das Hoheitszeichen*) of the eagle with outstretched wings clutching in its claws a swastika (*Hakenkreuz*) surrounded by a wreath, and the circular cap cockade (*die deutsche Reichskokarde*). Officers' caps had silver piping around the crown, while generals had gold piping.

German: Pub. anon. Value B.

270. A sailor

This young *Matrose* (ordinary seaman) wears the blue pullover shirt, (*Bluse*) with its cornflower blue white-banded collar, and black silk tie. Over it he wears the service dress uniform jacket (*Dienstjacke*) with nine buttons down each side, which was fastened by a chain link. He wears the white summer cap (which was worn with white trousers), with the national emblem and cockade. It bears the name of his ship: *Panzer-schiff Deutschland*. Commissioned in 1933, she was the first of the new 'pocket battleships' to be built in Germany after the Treaty of Versailles limited the Kriegsmarine tonnage. She had seen service during the Spanish Civil War, when some of her crew had been killed by a communist bomb off the Spanish coast. In February 1940 her name was changed to *Lützow* (the cruiser of that name having been sold to Russia). This undated photograph can therefore be placed at pre-1940. The sailor's name is O. Wolf.

German: Pub. and photographer anon. Value B.

Zur Erinnerung an unseren lieben, unvergeßlichen Sohn
Gren. Stefan Heuhsler
geb. 24. Dezember 1904, der am 2. August 1943 bei einer
Gefechtsübung tödlich verunglückt ist.

271   272   273

271. Two Sailors

These two sailors, photographed on shore on 15 April 1944 (much to the interest of passers-by) wear the standard pea jacket (*Überzieher*) with ordinary seamen's collar patches. This warm, thick, woolen navy blue jacket, was worn by all ranks as a greatcoat. Underneath they wear the standard pullover. The legend on their winter caps is simply '*Kriegsmarine*'. The pre-war caps which actually bore the name of a sailor's ship, were all supposed to have been withdrawn when war broke out, although one occasionally sees wartime photographs with named hat bands. The sailor on the left is wearing the Destroyer Badge on his left-hand side. This badge was first awarded to men who had engaged in the Battle of Narvik in June 1940. The winners had either to have been wounded in action or sunk, engaged in several enemy actions, served in twelve sorties, or served with distinction or merit. The message on the reverse, for security reasons, only gives the phrase 'In Westerns' – on the Western Front.
German: Pub. and photographer anon. Value B.

272. Gren. Stefan Heuhsler

The mourning card translates 'In memory of our beloved, unforgettable son, Grenadier Stefan Heuhsler, born 24 December 1904, who on 2 August 1943 died in a fatal accident in combat practice'.
German Pub. and photographer anon. Value B.

273. Pipsi

The message on the reverse records that 'Pipsi' joined up on 30 October 1940, went on active service on 10 February 1941, and was killed in Russia on 5 March 1942.
German: Pub. and photographer anon. Value B.

[120]

Index

▼————————————▼